COMPACT *Research*

Coal Power

Peggy J. Parks

Energy and the Environment

ReferencePoint
Press®

San Diego, CA

About the Author

Peggy J. Parks holds a bachelor of science degree from Aquinas College in Grand Rapids, Michigan, where she graduated magna cum laude. She has written more than 80 nonfiction educational books for children and young adults, as well as published her cookbook *Welcome Home: Recipes, Memories, and Traditions from the Heart.* Parks lives in Muskegon, Michigan, a town that she says inspires her writing because of its location on the shores of Lake Michigan.

For more information, contact:
ReferencePoint Press, Inc.
PO Box 27779
San Diego, CA 92198
www. ReferencePointPress.com

Picture credits:
Cover: iStockphoto.com
Maury Aaseng: 31–34, 46–48, 60–62, 76–79
iStockphoto.com: 10, 14

LIBRARY OF CONGRESS CATALOGING-IN-PUBLICATION DATA

Parks, Peggy J., 1951–
   Coal power / by Peggy J. Parks.
     p. cm. — (Compact research series)
   Includes bibliographical references and index.
   ISBN-13: 978-1-60152-107-1 (hbk.)
   ISBN-10: 1-60152-107-3 (hbk.)
   1. Coal trade—Juvenile literature. 2. Coal-fired power plants--Juvenile literature. 3. Coal—Juvenile literature. 4. Power resources--Juvenile literature. I. Title.
   HD9540.5.P37 2009
   363.738—dc22

                             2009040878

Contents

Foreword

❝Where is the knowledge we have lost in information?❞

—T.S. Eliot, "The Rock."

As modern civilization continues to evolve, its ability to create, store, distribute, and access information expands exponentially. The explosion of information from all media continues to increase at a phenomenal rate. By 2020 some experts predict the worldwide information base will double every 73 days. While access to diverse sources of information and perspectives is paramount to any democratic society, information alone cannot help people gain knowledge and understanding. Information must be organized and presented clearly and succinctly in order to be understood. The challenge in the digital age becomes not the creation of information, but how best to sort, organize, enhance, and present information.

ReferencePoint Press developed the *Compact Research* series with this challenge of the information age in mind. More than any other subject area today, researching current issues can yield vast, diverse, and unqualified information that can be intimidating and overwhelming for even the most advanced and motivated researcher. The *Compact Research* series offers a compact, relevant, intelligent, and conveniently organized collection of information covering a variety of current topics ranging from illegal immigration and deforestation to diseases such as anorexia and meningitis.

The series focuses on three types of information: objective single-author narratives, opinion-based primary source quotations, and facts and statistics. The clearly written objective narratives provide context and reliable background information. Primary source quotes are carefully selected and cited, exposing the reader to differing points of view. And facts and statistics sections aid the reader in evaluating perspectives. Presenting these key types of information creates a richer, more balanced learning experience.

For better understanding and convenience, the series enhances information by organizing it into narrower topics and adding design features that make it easy for a reader to identify desired content. For example, in *Compact Research: Illegal Immigration*, a chapter covering the economic impact of illegal immigration has an objective narrative explaining the various ways the economy is impacted, a balanced section of numerous primary source quotes on the topic, followed by facts and full-color illustrations to encourage evaluation of contrasting perspectives.

The ancient Roman philosopher Lucius Annaeus Seneca wrote, "It is quality rather than quantity that matters." More than just a collection of content, the *Compact Research* series is simply committed to creating, finding, organizing, and presenting the most relevant and appropriate amount of information on a current topic in a user-friendly style that invites, intrigues, and fosters understanding.

Coal Power at a Glance

Types of Coal

The four main types of coal are lignite, sub-bituminous, bituminous, and anthracite. Lignite is the softest and contains the lowest amount of carbon, while anthracite is the hardest and has as much as 95 percent carbon content.

Coal Supplies

The United States, Russia, India, China, Australia, and South Africa have about 85 percent of the world's coal. The top coal-producing U.S. states are Wyoming, West Virginia, Kentucky, Pennsylvania, Montana, and Texas.

World Dependence

People all over the world rely on coal, especially for generating electricity. Coal is also burned in factories that make steel, cement, and paper, among other products.

Acid Rain

Coal burning releases pollutants such as sulfur and nitrogen into the atmosphere. These pollutants interact with water vapor to form acid rain.

Global Warming

Emissions from the burning of coal pump billions of tons of the heat-trapping gas carbon dioxide (CO_2) into the air. CO_2 is considered to be a major contributor to global warming.

Mining's Impact on the Environment

Most coal in the United States is retrieved through surface mining, which can irreparably harm land, water, and wildlife. The most destructive type is mountaintop removal mining, where mountains are blasted apart so that deep coal seams can be reached.

Growing Demand

Even though coal is a finite resource, meaning it will eventually be depleted, the use of coal is expected to rise in the coming decades. The most dramatic increases are projected for developing countries such as China and India.

Overview

For most people, especially those who live in industrialized countries, life without electricity would be unimaginable. Simple things,
such as turning on lights, keeping food refrigerated, heating food
in the microwave, or flipping a switch that starts coffee brewing, would
not be possible without electrical power. Although coal may not be on
people's minds when they enjoy these conveniences, it plays a major role
in electrical generation because it is the primary source of fuel for power
plants in the United States, China, and a number of other countries. The
American Coal Council, which represents the U.S. coal industry, says
that coal is the most abundant and the least expensive of any fuel source,
which means it is the best choice for cheap, reliable electricity. "Whereas
people in developing nations still often rely on open fires and physical
effort to power their homes and drive their industry," the group states,
"people in developed countries rely on automation and electrical power.
With electricity, we North Americans heat our homes, power our com-

puters, charge our cell phones and operate our appliances. With it, we also power the production of a myriad of consumer products. The need for abundant, inexpensive electricity has become an essential aspect of the North American lifestyle. . . . Using coal just makes sense."[1]

An Ancient Fuel Source

Coal, along with crude oil and natural gas, is known as a fossil fuel because it formed from the fossilized remains of ancient vegetation. This process began hundreds of millions of years ago during the Carboniferous period, a time when the climate was extremely warm and humid and much of the earth was covered with vast, swampy areas. Soft, pulpy trees, ferns, and other lush plants thrived in the swamps, and after this vegetation died, it fell into the water and began to decompose. Over the millions of years that passed, layers upon layers of clay, sand, gravel, and sediment covered the decomposing material and squeezed it tightly together. At first, a thick layer of spongy material known as peat began to form beneath the layers. As the layers continued to grow deeper and heavier, the peat was compressed even more tightly, which subjected it to high temperatures and tremendous pressure. This caused chemical changes to take place that eventually transformed the organic material into coal.

> Coal, along with crude oil and natural gas, is known as a fossil fuel because it formed from the fossilized remains of ancient vegetation.

A Brief History of Coal Power

There is no way to know with any certainty when humans first discovered coal, although many scientists and historians believe that it was used during ancient times. In their book *Coal Combustion and Gasification*, L. Douglas Smoot and Philip J. Smith write: "Direct combustion of coal has been identified in some of the earliest recorded history."[2] The authors make reference to historical books saying the Chinese used coal as early as 1000 B.C., while the Greeks and Romans made use of coal before 200 B.C. Historians say that by A.D. 1215, coal trade had started in England.

Smoke pours from the towers of a coal-burning power plant. Coal burning releases pollutants and the heat-trapping gas carbon dioxide, linked to global warming, into the air. Despite these hazards, coal power plays a central role in meeting the world's energy needs.

The American Coal Foundation states that during the 1300s in what is now the United States, Native Americans used coal for cooking and heating and to bake the pottery that they shaped from clay.

According to the Energy Information Administration, coal was first discovered in the United States in 1673 along the Illinois River in northern Illinois. The find was recorded on a map that was drawn by French Canadian explorer Louis Joliet, who referred to *charbon de terre,* meaning "coal of the earth." In 1701 coal was found in Virginia, and over the following decades it was also discovered in Pennsylvania, Ohio, Kentucky, West Virginia, and Wyoming, as well as other states.

For a number of years wood was the primary fuel used for burning, and coal was considered a secondary fuel source. Then during the mid-1880s, rapid deforestation became a concern, which led to a greater reliance on coal. An especially significant factor in the expansion of coal use was the Industrial Revolution, a period of rapid industrial growth that began in Britain during the last half of the eighteenth century and spread to the United States in the 1800s. As the demand for energy continued to grow, the use of coal began to soar. Because coal was plentiful as well as cheap, it was burned to power textile mills and factories and was also used to heat water in huge boilers on ships and railroad trains that were powered by steam. By the end of the 1800s, coal was being used by power plants to generate electricity.

> **An especially significant factor in the expansion of coal use was the Industrial Revolution, a period of rapid industrial growth that began in Britain during the last half of the eighteenth century and spread to the United States in the 1800s.**

Types of Coal

There are 4 main types of coal: lignite, sub-bituminous, bituminous, and anthracite, each of which contains varying amounts of carbon. Lignite (also called brown coal), the youngest and softest of all coal types, is brownish black in color and very crumbly. It contains only 25 to 35 percent carbon and has the highest water content of all the coal types. Because lignite is so soft, its main use is burning to create steam that produces electricity. Sub-bituminous coal is medium soft, contains much less moisture than lignite, and has a carbon content of about 35 to 45 percent. It is also primarily used to produce steam for coal-fired power plants. Bituminous coal contains even less moisture than sub-bituminous, and it has a carbon content that ranges from 45 to 85 percent. It, too, is used to generate electricity, as well as to produce coke, a coal by-product that is used in the steel industry. Anthracite is the oldest type of coal and has the highest carbon content, as much as 95 percent. Because it is also the hardest, anthracite burns hotter and more slowly than other types of coal, so it makes the best heating fuel.

> **The U.S. Department of Energy states that more than 90 percent of the coal used in the United States is for electricity generation, with coal providing more than half of the country's electrical power.**

Where Coal Is Located

Although coal is found on every continent, including Antarctica, an estimated 85 percent of the world's coal reserves are in 6 countries: the United States, the Russian Federation, India, China, Australia, and South Africa. (Reserves are defined as coal supplies that have been discovered and are recoverable from the earth.) According to the Energy Information Administration, the United States has an estimated 30 percent of global coal reserves, and coal is mined in 26 states. Since 1988 Wyoming has been the top coal-producing state in the country, followed by West Virginia, Kentucky, Pennsylvania, Montana, and Texas. Of all the coal types, anthracite is the scarcest, accounting for less than 0.5 percent of the coal mined in the United States, with all anthracite mines located in Pennsylvania. America's most plentiful type of coal is bituminous, which is primarily mined in West Virginia, Kentucky, and Illinois. Sub-bituminous coal is found west of the Mississippi River, with the greatest amounts in Wyoming and Montana. Lignite is found primarily in Montana, Texas, and North Dakota.

How Dependent Is the World on Coal Power?

Today countries throughout the world depend on coal, especially for the generation of electricity. The U.S. Department of Energy states that more than 90 percent of the coal used in the United States is for electricity generation, with coal providing more than half of the country's electrical power. In other countries, especially in Asia, people depend on coal even more for their electricity. China, for instance, is the world's largest consumer of coal, using it to generate as much as 80 percent of the country's electricity. India's dependence on coal for electricity has grown in recent years and is expected to continue to increase. Poland and several other European countries also generate the largest share of their electricity from coal-fired power plants.

In addition to producing electrical power, coal has many other uses. According to the Stowe Global Coal Index, a performance measurement for the coal industry, approximately 64 percent of steel production worldwide comes from iron made in blast furnaces that burn coal. Coal is also used in cement production, aluminum refineries, paper manufacturing, and the chemical and pharmaceutical industries. The American Coal Foundation adds that the chemicals methanol and ethylene, which can be made from coal gas, are used to make products such as plastics, medicines, fertilizers, and tar.

> " Throughout the world, acid rain has killed forests and other vegetation and destroyed wildlife habitats. "

Does Coal Burning Threaten the Environment?

In spite of coal's innumerable uses, coal power is a topic of widespread controversy. Whenever it is burned, pollutants are emitted into the atmosphere through power plants' huge smokestacks. Two examples are sulfur and nitrogen, which chemically interact with oxygen to form compounds known as oxides. When oxides combine with water vapor in the air (such as in clouds), highly corrosive acids known as sulfuric acid and nitric acid are formed, and this can result in a destructive form of pollution known as acid rain. It falls to the earth in the form of rain, snow, sleet, fog, or dry particles and ends up on land and in bodies of water, as well as on structures such as buildings, historic monuments, and bridges.

Trains such as this one crisscross the country, carrying coal to power plants. Mindful of the world's reliance on coal power, scientists are working on ways to make coal burn more cleanly and emit fewer pollutants and less carbon dioxide into the atmosphere.

Throughout the world, acid rain has killed forests and other vegetation and destroyed wildlife habitats. Some of the worst damage in the United States has occurred in the Adirondack Mountains in northeastern New York. According to the Adirondack Council, more than 700 lakes and ponds have become too acidic to support their native aquatic wildlife. The group describes other damage:

> Heritage strains of brook trout have gone extinct. Thousands of acres of high-elevation forests have been killed. Mercury pollution from the same coal-fired power plant smokestacks is poisoning fish, birds and mammals. The Catskill Mountains, Hudson Highlands, Long Island's eastern Pine Barrens and the Finger Lakes are also suffering long-term damage from acid rain. Acid rain damages East Coast ecosystems from the Florida Everglades to the forests of Maine.[3]

In addition to acid rain, another controversy exists over the amount of CO_2 that is emitted into the atmosphere whenever coal is burned. CO_2 is a gas that is essential for life. Plants take it from the air during photosynthesis, the process by which they combine energy from the sun with CO_2 and water to produce their food. Another vital function performed by CO_2 is its powerful heat-trapping ability, whereby the gas traps and holds the sun's heat and keeps the earth warm enough for living things. Yet that same quality, many scientists say, is contributing to an unusually rapid warming of the planet's temperature known as global warming. Although it is a naturally occurring gas, measurements have shown that the amount of CO_2 in the atmosphere has increased by an estimated 30 percent since the beginning of the Industrial Revolution. Since CO_2 is one of the major greenhouse gases, those who are most concerned about

> " According to a June 2009 report by British Petroleum (BP), worldwide demand for coal in 2008 was the highest of all fuels for the sixth consecutive year. "

global warming are convinced that human activities, such as the burning of fossil fuels, are responsible for the higher temperatures. If global temperatures continue to rise, scientists warn, it could have catastrophic effects on the planet.

What Are the Environmental Effects of Coal Mining?

Years ago when coal was much more plentiful than it is today, it was mined underground. Mines were drilled deep into the earth, and miners rode elevators down to shafts where they operated machines that dug out the coal. Then huge conveyer belts carried the coal back up to the surface. Although more than half of the coal worldwide comes from underground mining, this method is being used less frequently in the United States. In many areas of the country, such as in the Appalachian region, coal can no longer be reached by underground mining, either because it is buried too deep or because underground mines would be too narrow and dangerous for workers. The National Mining Association states that an estimated 70 percent of the coal in the United States is now mined using surface mining methods such as strip mining. Of all the methods used to mine coal, this is by far the most destructive to the environment.

> The issue of the world's remaining coal reserves is often debated, with some scientists insisting that there is enough coal to last for several hundred more years, and others predicting that it will run out much sooner than people think.

During the process of strip mining, coal miners use enormous, earth-moving shovels to break up and remove tons of rock and topsoil, which the coal industry refers to as "spoil" or "overburden." With the top layers removed, the coal beds are blasted apart with dynamite—and when this occurs on mountaintops (known as mountaintop removal mining), entire mountains are literally blown apart so thin seams of coal buried below can be reached. Once the coal has been exposed, it is scooped up and loaded onto trucks or railroad cars for transport. Then the overburden, which is considered waste material, is dumped into valleys, lagoons, and streams.

In 2006 Tracy Shapiro, who writes for the publication *Appalachian Voice*, investigated Looney Creek, which is located on Black Mountain in Virginia. Shapiro was distraught by the extent of the damage caused by coal mining in the area, as she explains:

> Impairment of water quality on such a vast scale is legal only because of a federal administrative interpretation of the Clean Water Act that allows mining companies to get away with it. Legal or not, it is surely wrong to kill these streams—as hundreds of miles of such streams have been killed or buried in recent years by strip mining in Appalachia—a crime against nature and against the people who live here and downstream. . . . If there is to be any future for nature or human beings in this part of the world, this must stop.[4]

Growing Worldwide Demand

According to a June 2009 report by British Petroleum (BP), worldwide demand for coal in 2008 was the highest of all fuels for the sixth consecutive year. China's use of coal continues to increase rapidly, and the country's energy demand is projected to be as much as 85 percent greater by the year 2030 than it is today. Coal consumption is also on the rise in some European countries. An April 2008 article in the *New York Times* states that within 5 years, Italy plans to increase its reliance on coal from 14 percent to 33 percent, and coal consumption is expected to grow in Germany and Britain as well. In the United States coal usage is expected to remain about the same or perhaps decrease slightly, but U.S. coal exports to other countries will likely rise.

Coal Depletion

The issue of the world's remaining coal reserves is often debated, with some scientists insisting that there is enough coal to last for several hundred more years, and others predicting that it will run out much sooner than people think. According to a June 2009 report by British Petroleum, worldwide coal reserves total about 910 billion tons (826 billion metric tons). Scientist David Rutledge disagrees, however, saying that the figure is too high. Rutledge studied trends in regions throughout the world that have already run out of coal, and he found that coal reserves are closer to 660 billion tons (600 billion metric tons). He speculates that worldwide production of coal could begin to peak as early as 2025.

> **Even though coal is a finite resource, it is still far more plentiful than oil and natural gas, which means it is the cheapest of all fossil fuels.**

Whatever the correct estimate, coal is a finite resource that will eventually be used up. "It took hundreds of millions of years for fossil fuel reserves to form," says New York University physics professor Martin Hoffert, "and we're using them up a million times faster than nature made them! As the worldwide demand for energy continues to grow, these fuels are being removed from the ground at an increasingly rapid rate—and when they're gone, they're gone."[5]

What Is the Future of Coal Power?

Since the world is dependent on coal for so many uses, it will likely remain a major power source throughout the coming decades. Even though coal is a finite resource, it is still far more plentiful than oil and natural gas, which means it is the cheapest of all fossil fuels. But because it is known for polluting the air and water, scientists are developing ways to help decrease the toxic emissions that power plants send into the atmosphere. One method is known as flue gas desulfurization. Power plants built in the United States after 1978 are required by federal law to have special devices that clean the sulfur from the coal's combustion gases before the gases go up the smokestack. The U.S. Department of Energy explains: "The technical name for these devices is 'flue gas desulfurization units,' but most people just call them 'scrubbers'—because they 'scrub' the sulfur out of the smoke released by coal-burning boilers."[6]

Several European countries, including Britain, Germany, and Italy, are planning to convert a number of power plants from oil to coal in the coming years. Many will feature clean coal technologies, in which efforts have been taken to reduce the emission of pollutants such as sulfur dioxide and nitrogen oxides. Italy's primary motivation for relying on coal is cost, because fuel prices have risen more than 150 percent since 1996, and Italian citizens pay the highest electricity rates in Europe. The energy company Enel is constructing a coal-fired power plant in Civitavecchia, Italy, that it says will be the cleanest in all of Europe. As Enel's chief of energy generation and management explains: "We are hoping to prove that it will be possible to make sustainable and environmentally friendly use of coal."[7] In addition to having scrubber technology, the Civitavecchia facility will chemically convert its nitrous oxide into ammonia, which will then be sold to industries that use it in the production of products such as agricultural fertilizer and livestock feed. The plant will also recycle its waste coal ash by selling it to manufacturers who use it as a raw material to produce cement. Another feature is an on-site desalination plant that will remove salt from seawater so the facility can generate its own water for cooling without tapping into freshwater supplies. The heated water that comes out of the plant will be used for heating one of Italy's largest fish farms.

The Uncertainty Lingers

Coal is an indispensable fuel for countries all over the world. From electricity generation to the manufacture of steel, cement, and many consumer products, people have long relied on coal, and this is expected to continue over the coming decades. There are challenges associated with coal, however. It is a finite resource, which means that supplies will someday be depleted. Both coal mining and coal burning are damaging to the environment. As scientists continue to search for new coal resources and develop new technology that helps reduce coal's environmental impact, some of these obstacles may eventually be overcome.

How Dependent Is the World on Coal Power?

66We should do more to increase energy conservation efforts. We should choose natural gas over coal to meet short-term needs. We should stop building new coal-fired power plants.99

—Chester Sansbury, the South Carolina coordinator for Republicans for Environmental Protection.

66Why the opposition to coal? After all, the U.S. is energy independent with respect to this resource, with 275 billion tons in proven reserves, which is more than enough to meet our energy needs for hundreds of years.99

—Ronald Bailey, science correspondent for *Reason* magazine.

Wu Yiebing and his wife, Cao Waiping, feel very fortunate that they have a good life in the small town of Hanjing, China. Wu earns about $200 per month operating a large drill in an underground coal mine, and the job has made it possible for him and his wife to enjoy a modern lifestyle. They live in a brick house with conveniences such as a refrigerator, stereo, television, telephone, and electric lights. For people living in Western countries who are used to far more luxuries, the Wu family's possessions may not seem like much. But their current way of life is a vast improvement over the past, when they lived in a mud hut in the mountain village where they both grew up. Electricity was only available for a few hours each evening when water from a nearby dam was released to turn a small turbine. On hillside terraces that were too small to accommodate tractors, Wu and Cao farmed the land by hand. And with an income of just $25 per month, they could barely afford anything to eat besides rice. Today prosperity they could only dream about years ago has been made possible because of coal and the electrical power it generates.

A Fast-Growing Economy

Of all the countries in the world that rely on coal, China depends on it the most by far. Currently, the country uses coal to generate more of its power than the United States, the European Union, and Japan combined. Since 1996 consumption of electricity in China has grown by 175 percent, and its demand for electrical power is expected to keep increasing by an estimated 10 percent each year. According to the World Coal Institute, coal has made it possible to provide electricity to more than 450 million Chinese people over a 15-year period. Yet China is still considered a developing country, with 10 million citizens who have no electricity. "In rural areas," states a May 2007 National Public Radio report, "many children have never seen an electric light." In order to expand electrical power throughout the country, Chinese officials intend to construct an additional 500 coal-fired power plants by 2017—a rate of nearly 1 per week. But these new plants will do much more than bring electrical power to rural villages, as the National Public Radio story explains: "They're also powering the factories that make up China's exploding manufacturing base. In the past year, China has added generating capacity that is equal to the whole of France's electricity grid."[8]

> " Currently, [China] uses coal to generate more of its power than the United States, the European Union, and Japan combined. "

The expansion of coal-fired power plants has helped China's economy immensely. Experts say that since 1979, when the country opened its economy to worldwide trade, Chinese exports increased from $14 billion to $1,429 billion. During the first and second quarters of 2009, the total value of China's goods and services produced (known as gross domestic product) rose by nearly 8 percent, and it became the first major economy to rebound from the worldwide recession.

One of the newest factories in China is located in the middle of the Ordos Desert, an area that borders northern China's Inner Mongolia region and Shaanxi Province. Approved for construction by the Chinese government in 2002 and operational by December 2008, the factory converts solid coal into liquid fuels such as diesel fuel and liquefied natural gas. Coal liquefaction plants like this one boost China's ability to support itself. Currently, China depends on imports for about 50 percent of its crude oil. Zhang Xiwu, who is chair of China's biggest coal producer, Shenhua Group, explains why this facility and others like it are so important. "I feel it a must for China to master the technology, as the country needs more and more liquid fuels, most of which are imported. The pirates along the oil transportation routes and the political changes in the Middle East are affecting our imports. The fuel we produce out of coal could be an important source of strategic oil reserves to ensure energy security."[9] Zhang adds that the technology featured in the facility could raise coal efficiency at least fivefold, with a production process that features almost zero pollution.

> " Approved for construction by the Chinese government in 2002 and operational by December 2008, the factory converts solid coal into liquid fuels such as diesel fuel and liquefied natural gas. "

Helping India Prosper

Another Asian country that is growing increasingly dependent on coal is India. According to an August 2009 report by the Center for Strategic and International Studies' South Asia Program, coal is India's primary fuel source. It accounted for 53 percent of the country's energy consumption during 2007, and demand "is set to grow dramatically over the coming decades." The report adds that coal use for electricity generation in India is projected to grow 2 percent each year, nearly doubling its share of the country's current generating capacity by 2030. The authors state: "This will increase not only domestic production but also imports: Over the next two decades, coal imports are projected to triple compared with the 2007 level."[10]

The steep rise in India's demand for coal results from economic growth, as well as the government's policies to assist the country's poorest citizens. Currently, 400 million people in rural areas of India do not have access to electricity. Government officials have created programs that either heavily subsidize fuel costs or provide free electricity to citizens living in various rural areas. In order to meet the growing demand for electricity, the government and its coal ministry plan to increase the production of electrical power by an estimated 65 percent over the next 10 years.

Europe's Reliance on Coal

The World Coal Institute states that a number of European countries depend on coal for their electrical power. One of these countries is Britain, where about one-third of all electricity is generated by coal-fired power plants. During the 1980s and 1990s, new sources of oil and natural gas were discovered in the North Sea, which caused British coal usage to decline. But according to a March 2008 article in the *Washington Post*, that trend has reversed, and "coal consumption has climbed steadily over the past six years, including a 9 percent jump from 2005 to 2006. Coal has now surpassed gas once again as the leading fuel for [Britain's] electricity plants."[11] Because of reduced mine production capacity since the 1990s, Britain now imports more than 65 percent of its coal from Russia, Colombia, and South Africa.

Poland depends on coal for a

> " The steep rise in India's demand for coal results from economic growth, as well as the government's policies to assist the country's poorest citizens. "

much larger portion of its electricity than Britain. The country has an estimated 140 years of coal resources left and is the eighth leading coal producer and exporter in the world. According to a September 2009 article published in *Your Mining News*, Poland's coal-fired power generation system is the largest in central and eastern Europe in terms of capacity. The country's 38 million people depend on coal for more than 90 to 95 percent of their electricity—the highest in the European Union. Richard Cordoba, president of Western Europe and North Africa GE Energy, explains: "Coal continues to have a major role in meeting the need for reliable and affordable electricity in Poland and throughout Europe."[12]

Coal's Growing Importance in Turkey

Another country that depends on coal for much of its electrical power is Turkey. Although Turkey has an abundance of coal reserves, not enough is mined to meet the country's demand, so it relies on imported coal for more than half of its consumption. Coal imports primarily come from Australia, the United States, South Africa, and Russia. To add to the 15 existing coal-fired power plants, Turkish officials plan to construct nearly 50 new plants in the coming years. One huge coal-fired power plant is located just outside the Turkish town of Iskenderun, on the coastline of the Mediterranean Sea. This plant alone produces about 5 percent of Turkey's total electricity.

> **Although Turkey has an abundance of coal reserves, not enough is mined to meet the country's demand, so it relies on imported coal for more than half of its consumption.**

Along with electricity generation, Turkey also relies on coal to power its manufacturing plants, such as those that produce cement. The country's population has soared over the past decades, from just 13 million in 1927 to nearly 77 million in 2009. Along with that population growth came the construction of numerous highways and bridges, which caused a steep rise in the demand for cement. Today Turkey is one of the 10 largest cement-producing countries in the world. It is also a world leader in steel production, and coal is used to power those factories as well. In 2008 Turkey was ranked eleventh in the world for all steel-producing countries. One enormous steel mill is located in the town of Isdemir, Turkey. It employs about 6,000 people and produces nearly 6 million tons (5.4 million metric tons) of steel per year.

Coal in the United States

With an estimated 30 percent of global coal reserves, the United States is richer in coal than any other country in the world. America relies heavily on coal, primarily for electricity generation, but also for powering manufacturing plants. In 2008 U.S. coal consumption was more than 1 billion tons (907 million metric tons), and according to a July 2009 report by the Missouri coal producer Arch Coal, 94 percent of that was used to produce electrical power. The rest of the coal was consumed by the industrial, commercial, metal production, and residential sectors. Arch Coal chair and chief executive officer Steven Leer says that coal is a vital part of America's energy needs and will become even more so as the demand for energy continues to increase. "The trends are unstoppable," he says. "The question is how we meet our energy demands. I think we will need all our energy sources."[13]

Coal is also important to the United States because of the revenue from exports to other countries. "Many countries do not have natural energy resources sufficient to cover their energy needs," the World Coal Institute writes, "and therefore need to import energy to help meet their requirements. Japan, Chinese Taipei and Korea, for example, import significant quantities of steam coal for electricity generation and . . . coal for steel production."[14] According to a March 2008 *Washington Post* article, the boom in coal exports helped lower America's trade deficit (imports higher than exports), which declined in 2007 for the first time since 2001. The value of coal exports, which account for 2.5 percent of all U.S. exports, grew by 19 percent during 2007, and even bigger increases are expected in the coming years.

The importance of coal in the United States was the subject of a July 2009 presentation by Don Nehlen, a former West Virginia University football coach who is now a spokesperson for the coal industry. Nehlen was asked what the effects would be if the U.S. government tried to phase out America's dependence on coal, to which he replied: "If that would disappear, we'd be in a heap of hurt. And not only would West

Virginia, but so would America. I mean, 52 percent of the electricity generated in this country comes from coal. Ninety-eight percent generated in West Virginia comes from coal. Now, if there's enough windmills in the world to generate all that, I'd like to know where they're going to put them all."[15]

The strongest supporters of coal power say that a major reason coal is vital to the United States is the jobs it provides. A September 2009 report by the Energy Information Administration states that U.S. coal mines employed an average of 86,719 workers in 2008, including 49,575 employees at underground mines and 37,144 workers at surface mines. That was nearly a 7 percent increase over 2007, when U.S. coal mines employed just over 81,000 workers.

An Invaluable Resource

Because coal is more abundant than oil or natural gas, as well as much cheaper than either, it is a primary fuel source for countries throughout the world. Developing nations such as China and India depend on coal for electricity generation and manufacturing and to help them grow their economies. Industrialized nations consider coal to be one of the world's most important fuels, and their reliance on it is expected to grow as well. As global coal reserves continue to be depleted, the search for new sources of coal and more efficient technologies for using it will progress. In the face of rising demand, those efforts may be a crucial piece of meeting the world's energy needs.

How Dependent Is the World on Coal Power?

66 Just as modern life is unimaginable without electricity, so is the notion that we could meet our growing energy needs without coal. 99

—American Coalition for Clean Coal Electricity, "Issues & Policy," 2009. www.americaspower.org.

The American Coalition for Clean Coal Electricity seeks to advance the development of clean coal technologies for production of electricity.

66 There are many, more efficient alternatives to coal-fired power plants that can both guarantee our energy future and provide cleaner, healthier options for meeting our energy needs. 99

—Sierra Club, "Coal Questions & Answers," 2009. www.sierraclub.org.

The Sierra Club works to protect the planet, communities, and wild places.

Bracketed quotes indicate conflicting positions.

* Editor's Note: While the definition of a primary source can be narrowly or broadly defined, for the purposes of Compact Research, a primary source consists of: 1) results of original research presented by an organization or researcher; 2) eyewitness accounts of events, personal experience, or work experience; 3) first-person editorials offering pundits' opinions; 4) government officials presenting political plans and/or policies; 5) representatives of organizations presenting testimony or policy.

> **Cheap electricity promoted by the coal industry isn't cheap if it doesn't include the cost of protecting the health of the people and the planet.**

—Dave Skoloda, "'Dirty Coal' Not Really So Cheap," *Onalaska Holmen (WI) Courier-Life*, September 9, 2009. www.courierlifenews.com.

Skoloda is an adjunct professor of journalism at Winona State University in Minnesota.

> **Coal will remain the world's, the nation's and Ohio's energy work horse producing bulk, reliable, secure electric power at a reasonable cost.**

—Ohio Air Quality Development Authority, "The Ohio Coal Story," 2009. www.ohioairquality.org.

The Ohio Air Quality Development Authority's primary mission is to provide for the conservation of air as a natural resource in Ohio by preventing or reducing air pollution.

> **Coal is an extremely important fuel and will remain so. . . . Coal is the world's most abundant and widely distributed fossil fuel source.**

—World Nuclear Association, "'Clean Coal' Technologies, Carbon Capture & Sequestration," September 20, 2009. www.world-nuclear.org.

The World Nuclear Association promotes nuclear power as a sustainable energy resource worldwide.

> **Despite coal industry claims, U.S. coal power is neither 'abundant' nor 'cheap.' It's a sinking ship.**

—David Roberts, "Debate: Roberts v. 'Clean Coal' Flack Joe Lucas," *Huffington Post*, May 14, 2009. www.huffingtonpost.com.

Roberts is a senior writer for the environmental news blog Grist.

66 New renewable energy technologies, combined with a broad suite of energy-efficiency advances, will allow global energy needs to be met without fossil fuels. 99

—Christopher Flavin, "Low-Carbon Energy: A Roadmap," Worldwatch Institute, 2008. www.worldwatch.org.

Flavin is president of the Worldwatch Institute.

66 There is a good reason why coal has come to dominate the scene: It has been far and away the best way to generate electrical power. 99

—Victor Rudolph, "Let's Be Realistic About Coal," *Seed*, July 2, 2009. http://seedmagazine.com.

Rudolph is a professor of chemical engineering at the University of Queensland in Australia.

66 Coal has many important uses worldwide. The most significant uses are in electricity generation, steel production, cement manufacturing and as a liquid fuel. 99

—World Coal Institute, "Uses of Coal," 2009. www.worldcoal.org.

The World Coal Institute is an international organization representing the coal industry.

66 Coal reserves are crucial for providing global energy needs; more than 35 percent of our energy comes from coal and coal-fired plants. 99

—K.J. Reddy, "Give Clean Coal a Chance—and You Might Fry Bigger Fish," *Seed*, July 2, 2009. http://seedmagazine.com.

Reddy is a professor at the School of Energy Resources at the University of Wyoming.

How Dependent Is the World on Coal Power?

- About **85 percent** of global coal reserves are located in six countries: the United States, Russia, India, China, Australia, and South Africa.

- The United States and Russia combined account for nearly **50 percent** of total worldwide coal reserves.

- China only has **half the coal reserves** of the United States, but is the **world's largest coal producer**.

- **Wyoming** is America's top coal-producing state, and **Texas** is the country's top coal-consuming state.

- Solar Energy International states that approximately **2 billion** people worldwide have no electricity.

- China is the largest coal consumer in the world at **42 percent** of the total, followed by the United States at **16 percent**.

- Together, China, the United States, India, Japan, and Russia account for **72 percent** of total global coal use.

- An estimated **94 percent** of the total coal consumed in the United States is for electricity generation.

Global Coal Consumption

People all over the world depend on coal, primarily for electricity generation but also for manufacturing products such as steel, cement, and paper. This chart shows the countries that are the largest global coal consumers, with China at the top of the list because of its rapidly growing industry.

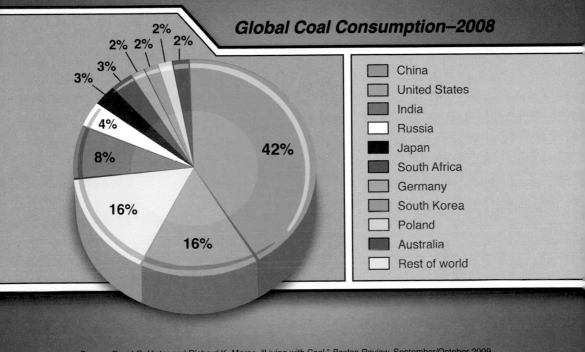

Global Coal Consumption—2008

Legend:
- China
- United States
- India
- Russia
- Japan
- South Africa
- Germany
- South Korea
- Poland
- Australia
- Rest of world

Pie chart values: 42%, 16%, 16%, 8%, 4%, 3%, 3%, 2%, 2%, 2%, 2%

Source: David G. Victor and Richard K. Morse, "Living with Coal," *Boston Review*, September/October 2009. http://bostonreview.net.

- The American Coalition for Clean Coal Electricity states that since 1970, the use of coal to generate electricity in the United States has nearly **tripled** in response to growing electricity demand.

- According to the World Coal Institute, coal is used to produce about **68 percent** of the total global production of steel.

Leading Coal-Producing States

According to the U.S. Energy Information Administration, coal is found in 26 states. It is most plentiful, however, in Wyoming, West Virginia, Kentucky, Pennsylvania, Montana, and Texas, which together produce more than 70 percent of total U.S. coal. This graph shows the top 10 states for coal production.

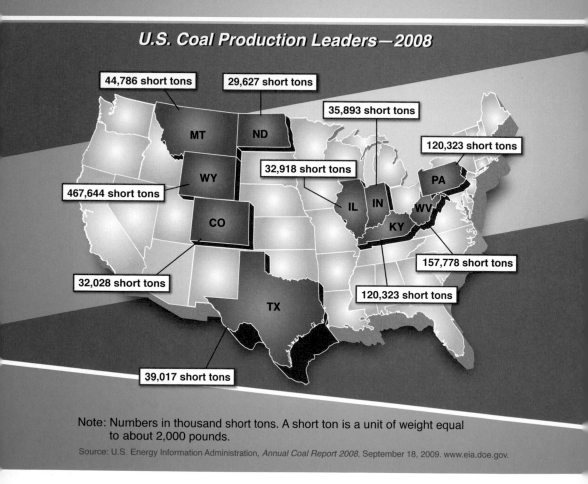

U.S. Coal Production Leaders—2008

- 44,786 short tons (MT)
- 29,627 short tons (ND)
- 35,893 short tons
- 120,323 short tons (PA)
- 32,918 short tons
- 467,644 short tons (WY)
- 157,778 short tons
- 32,028 short tons (CO)
- 120,323 short tons
- 39,017 short tons (TX)

Note: Numbers in thousand short tons. A short ton is a unit of weight equal to about 2,000 pounds.

Source: U.S. Energy Information Administration, *Annual Coal Report 2008*, September 18, 2009. www.eia.doe.gov.

- The Energy Information Administration states that the United States exports more coal to **Canada** than to any other country.

The World's Major Coal Exporters

With an estimated 30 percent of the world's reserves, the United States is richer in coal than any other country, yet in terms of coal exports five others rank higher. This graph shows the top 10 coal-exporting countries.

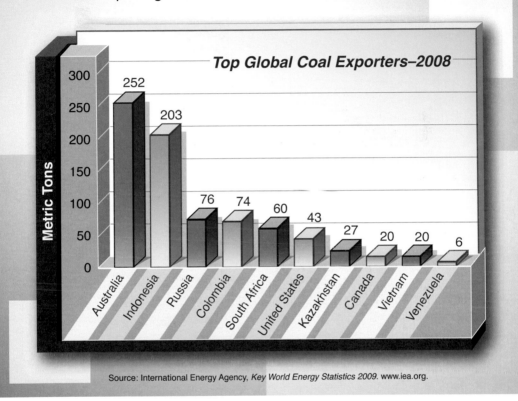

Top Global Coal Exporters–2008

Source: International Energy Agency, *Key World Energy Statistics 2009*. www.iea.org.

- China accounted for **two-thirds** of the more than **560** newly constructed coal-fired power plants worldwide between 2002 and 2006.

- A March 2009 article in Mining Weekly states that South Africa is dependent on coal for **90 percent** of its electricity.

- From August 2008 to August 2009, coal-fired electricity generation in the United States declined **9.4 percent**, while electricity generation from natural gas-fired plants increased **9.3 percent**.

Coal Is the Major Source of U.S. Electricity

People in the United States rely on coal for about half of all electricity that is generated. During 2008, coal-fired power plants produced more electricity than any other fuel source.

Electricity Generation by Fuel Source—2008

5% 6%

49%

20%

21%

| Coal | Natural gas | Nuclear | Hydroelectric | Other* |

*Includes wind, petroleum, wood, waste, geothermal, other gases, solar thermal and photovoltaic, batteries, chemicals, hydrogen, purchased steam, miscellaneous technologies, and non-renewable waste.

Note: Totals more than 100 percent due to rounding.

Source: U.S. Energy Information Administration, *Annual Energy Review 2008*, June 2009. www.eia.doe.gov.

- According to the Energy Information Administration, **617 facilities** in the United States burned coal to generate electricity in 2007, including 476 power plants and 141 industrial, commercial, and institutional facilities where most of the electricity generated was consumed on-site.

Does Coal Burning Threaten the Environment?

66 Coal is cheap, plentiful and dirty—as cheap as dirt, as plentiful as dirt, and as dirty as dirt—since after all, coal is little more than dirt that burns. 99

—Union of Concerned Scientists, a science-based nonprofit organization that works toward a healthy environment and a safer world.

66 Today's coal-based electricity generation is 70 to 90 percent cleaner than the plants that are being replaced—close to eliminating historical contributions to acid rain and smog. 99

—Hal Quinn, president and chief executive of the National Mining Association.

B y the early nineteenth century, people all over the world were relying on coal to provide them with electricity, keep factories operating, and heat their homes. Those who lived in large industrial cities often grew accustomed to the smokiness of the air and considered it to be an inevitable by-product of coal burning. There was little or no concern that the smoke might be harmful—but that changed on December 5, 1952, the date of one of the deadliest environmental catastrophes in history. It happened in London, England, where for weeks the weather had been significantly colder than what was typical for that time of year. To stay warm, people were burning larger-than-normal amounts of coal, and smoke billowed from chimneys and smokestacks all over

35

the city. The skies had been clear early that morning, but by nighttime, as temperatures dropped, fog began to roll in. As the normal fog mixed with soot in the air, the fog grew thick and dark. Stan Cribb, who was a funeral director in London at the time, says that even though he had witnessed many foggy days in London, nothing even came close to this.

"You had this swirling," he says, "like somebody had set a load of car tires on fire."[16]

> In the north-central part of China is Shanxi Province, one of the richest areas of the country for coal—and one of the most seriously polluted by coal-burning factories.

Within 2 days there was virtually no visibility in or around the city. People were walking blind through the streets, not even able see their feet. Although Cribb could tell that this was not normal fog, he had no way of knowing how dangerous it was. A mass of cold air had trapped toxic smoke from the coal fires near the ground, and the fog soon became thicker, blacker, and more poisonous. By December 10, when strong winds finally swept in and blew the fog off, more than 4,000 people had died. Thousands of others developed pneumonia, bronchitis, or other serious respiratory illnesses, and many of them died as well. Although there have been differing accounts about the final death toll, a study published in the journal *Environmental Health Perspectives* stated that as many as 12,000 people may have died from what came to be known as the "killer fog of 1952."

On the fiftieth anniversary of the catastrophe, National Public Radio did a special report on it, saying that "a mass of stagnant air . . . had clamped a lid over London, trapping the smoke from millions of residential coal fires at ground level. . . . In essence, the dead had suffocated."[17] Such a tragic event would be highly unlikely today because environmental laws in many countries have drastically cut down on the amount of soot and pollutants that can legally be emitted into the air. Yet coal pollution remains a problem in some parts of the world.

In the north-central part of China is Shanxi Province, one of the richest areas of the country for coal—and one of the most seriously polluted by coal-burning factories. Pollution extends throughout the entire province, including Datong, which has been named one of the most polluted cities in the world. A smoky haze filled with sulfur particles and other toxins hangs in the air, and by mid-afternoon each day it is so thick that drivers must turn on their cars' headlights to see. Houses and other buildings are covered in soot, as are vegetable stands and produce being sold along the roadsides. The same is true in neighboring Linfen. As a September 2007 report by the Blacksmith Institute states:

> Shanxi Province is at the heart of China's enormous and expanding coal industry, providing about two thirds of the nation's energy. Within this highly polluted region, Linfen has been identified as one of its most polluted cities with residents claiming that they literally choke on coal dust in the evenings. . . . The State Environmental Protection Administration (SEPA) has branded Linfen as having the worst air quality in the country. Levels of [sulfur dioxide] and other particulates are many times higher than limits set by the World Health Organization.[18]

Shanxi Province is not unique; pollution is a serious problem in much of China. The culprit, according to a 2008 Massachusetts Institute of Technology study of 85 power plants across 14 Chinese provinces, is coal. The institute researchers found that Chinese factories frequently use cheap, low-grade coal primarily to save money. According to the author of the study, "New market pressures encourage plant managers to buy the cheapest, lowest quality and most-polluting coal available, while at the same time idle expensive-to-operate smokestack scrubbers or other cleanup technologies."[19]

The Blacksmith Institute adds that of the 20 most polluted cities in the world, 16 are located in China, and this takes a heavy toll on public health. At least 400,000 premature deaths

> " **Another detrimental effect of coal burning in China is acid rain, which has destroyed an estimated one-third of the country's cropland.** "

each year are directly attributed to pollution-related illnesses. China has abnormally high rates of lung cancer and respiratory illnesses such as bronchitis and pneumonia. The Organization for Economic Co-Operation and Development predicts that by 2020, China will have 20 million cases of respiratory illness per year because of air pollution.

Acid Rain

Another detrimental effect of coal burning in China is acid rain, which has destroyed an estimated one-third of the country's cropland. Ancient structures have also been heavily damaged, such as the Marco Polo Bridge. Built in 1192, the bridge is so-named because it was mentioned by famed explorer Marco Polo in his account of his thirteenth-century trip to China. Five hundred stone lions adorn the bridge, and according to cultural expert Luo Zhewen, more than 20 percent have sustained serious damage due to acid rain. Luo adds that the engravings on many of the statues can no longer be seen clearly. Yet China's acid rain is not confined to China. The acid rain is a polluting "export" that drifts through the air and travels far beyond the country's borders. China is estimated to be responsible for nearly half of the acid rain in South Korea and Japan, which have sustained severe damage to their crops, forests, and water supplies.

> **Waste products generated by a coal-fired power plant in Harriman, Tennessee, led to one of the worst environmental disasters in U.S. history.**

In the United States acid rain was a serious problem in the past, and it did significant damage to lakes, streams, and forests. But under the Clean Air Act of 1990 and its acid rain amendment that took effect in 1995, there is now a permanent cap on the amount of sulfur dioxide and nitrogen oxide that can be emitted by electric power plants nationwide. The facilities must install scrubbers in their smokestacks; the scrubbers filter out these toxins before they enter the air. Although soil and water in some areas are still more acidic than what is normal, this is largely from damage that was done before the legislation was implemented. Today acid rain in the United States is much less of a problem than it was years ago.

Soot and Smog

One of the worst effects of burning coal is particle pollution, more commonly known as soot. The Sierra Club states that soot is the leading cause of haze and reduced visibility in the United States, including in the country's national parks. The group adds that the damage from this type of pollution continues after the soot has settled to the ground, "where it causes acidification of waters, soil nutrient depletion, and destruction of forests and crops."[20]

In January 2009 scientists from the U.S. Department of Energy's Pacific Northwest National Laboratory announced that soot is contributing to the premature melting of mountain snow in the western United States. After studying snowpacks in the Rocky Mountains and the Sierra Nevada and Cascade mountain ranges, the scientists found that soot that is carried through the air settles on the snow-covered mountains. It powders them with a dark layer that absorbs more sunlight than snow typically does, which causes the snow to melt weeks earlier than normal. The most serious effect of this early melting is the worsening of water shortages in areas that already face shortages every year. When snow melts earlier than usual, water that is stored in the mountains flows down streams and rivers in the spring and early summer. For states such as Wyoming that depend on snowmelt and its runoff into streams and reservoirs for water supplies, early snowmelt is a major problem. Climatologist Steve Gray explains: "When the snow melts earlier, then we don't get as much of the big flows that last us into the midsummer months."[21] Gray adds that without sufficient water for the midsummer months, Wyoming experiences summers that are hotter and drier than normal, and there is less water for crops and other uses.

Hazardous Waste

One of the by-products of coal-burning power plants is waste material, including ash and sludge from smokestack scrubbers. The Union of Concerned Scientists (UCS) states that a typical power plant produces more than 125,000 tons (113,400 metric tons) of ash and nearly 200,000 tons (181,000 metric tons) of sludge each year. This is typically disposed of in landfills and surface waste impoundments. The UCS adds that toxins in the waste include arsenic, mercury, chromium, and cadmium, which can contaminate drinking water supplies and endanger human health.

As the UCS states: "One study found that one out of every 100 children who drink groundwater contaminated with arsenic from coal power plant wastes were at risk of developing cancer. Ecosystems too have been damaged—sometimes permanently—by the disposal of coal plant waste."[22]

> Those who are most concerned about global warming warn that if CO_2 emissions are not sharply reduced, the planet will be irreparably damaged.

Waste products generated by a coal-fired power plant in Harriman, Tennessee, led to one of the worst environmental disasters in U.S. history. On December 22, 2008, a massive sludge impoundment burst, releasing hundreds of millions of gallons of coal waste into the surrounding area. The thick, gray sludge buried over 300 acres (121ha) of residential property and farmland near the coal plant, as well as spread through rivers and seeped into groundwater. A January 2009 article on the Intelligence Daily news site describes the damage:

> The spill killed a large number of fish, downed trees and power lines, destroyed an adjacent road and railway, ruptured a major gas line, and filled two inlets of the Emory River, which flows into the Clinch River and then into the Tennessee River—upon which millions of people depend for their drinking water. The flood rendered three homes uninhabitable—sweeping one totally off of its foundation—and damaged over 40 other residential properties, from which 22 families needed to be evacuated.[23]

Scientists say that the magnitude of the environmental damage in Harriman will likely not be known for years, and perhaps even decades.

Coal and Global Warming

Many scientists say that one of the biggest threats to the planet posed by coal power is global warming. Rising temperatures have already resulted in the melting of massive portions of sea ice and glaciers, diminishing snow on mountaintops, and melting permafrost in Arctic regions such as

Alaska and Siberia. Those who are most concerned about global warming warn that if CO_2 emissions are not sharply reduced, the planet will be irreparably damaged. One scientist who is particularly vocal in his concerns about global warming is James Hansen, the director of NASA's Goddard Institute for Space Studies. Hansen expressed his concern in a presentation given before Congress in June 2008: "Global warming initiated sea ice melt, exposing darker ocean that absorbs more sunlight, melting more ice. As a result, without any additional greenhouse gases, the Arctic soon will be ice-free in the summer."[24]

Because coal-fired power plants are a major source of CO_2 in the atmosphere, the growth of coal power in countries throughout the world is of concern to many scientists. One is David Hawkins, who is climate center director of the Natural Resources Defense Council in Washington, D.C. Referring to the prolific expansion of coal power in China, the United States, and other countries, Hawkins states: "These numbers show how far in the wrong direction the world is poised to go and indicate a lot of private sector investors still don't get it in terms of global warming. This rapid building of global-warming machines—which is what coal-power plants are—should be a wakeup call to politicians that we're driving ever faster toward the edge of the cliff."[25]

A Challenging Issue to Resolve

There is no question that coal burning adversely affects the environment in numerous ways. From soot pollution and acid rain to increasing amounts of CO_2 being pumped into the atmosphere, coal power threatens earth's air, water, and land, as well as human health. If these problems are ever to be overcome, it will be crucial for coal-consuming countries to find ways to reduce coal burning's environmental impact.

Does Coal Burning Threaten the Environment?

Primary Source Quotes

> **The trains carrying coal to power plants are death trains. Coal-fired power plants are factories of death.**

—James Hansen, "Coal-Fired Power Plants Are Death Factories. Close Them," *Guardian* (Manchester, UK), February 15, 2009. www.guardian.co.uk.

Hansen is the director of NASA's Goddard Institute for Space Studies and an adjunct professor in the Department of Earth and Environmental Sciences at Columbia University.

> **The alleged deaths from coal are based on speculative links between pollution and disease, and unwarranted extrapolations from responsible estimates to levels that generate headlines and contributions.**

—Paul Driessen, "Coal Power Saves Lives," *American Coal*, Spring 2009. www.clean-coal.info.

Driessen is the senior policy advisor for the Congress of Racial Equality and the Committee for a Constructive Tomorrow.

Bracketed quotes indicate conflicting positions.

* Editor's Note: While the definition of a primary source can be narrowly or broadly defined, for the purposes of Compact Research, a primary source consists of: 1) results of original research presented by an organization or researcher; 2) eyewitness accounts of events, personal experience, or work experience; 3) first-person editorials offering pundits' opinions; 4) government officials presenting political plans and/or policies; 5) representatives of organizations presenting testimony or policy.

❝Coal burning is to the environment what cigarette smoking is to the body.❞

—*Los Angeles Times*, "Coal Ash—a Tennessee Wake-Up Call," editorial, January 6, 2009. www.latimes.com.

The *Los Angeles Times* is the second-largest metropolitan newspaper in the United States.

❝Coal ash typically contains high concentrations of toxic chemicals like mercury, cadmium, and other heavy metals. Following the spill [in Tennessee], local television and photographers captured large numbers of dead fish washed up on the shores of the river and images of the area covered in mud and ash.❞

—Greenpeace, "Greenpeace Calls for Criminal Investigation into Coal Ash Spill," news release, December 23, 2008. www.greenpeace.org.

Greenpeace is an activist organization that works to expose environmental problems throughout the world and propose solutions that help solve them.

❝Coal ash is not toxic. . . . Fly ash, the substance that spilled in Tennessee, has an elemental composition comparable to the soil in the average American's backyard. Unless we're willing to sift up every yard in America, perhaps journalists ought to ponder the meaning of 'toxic.'❞

—Melissa Hendricks, "Coal Ash Is Not Toxic, Staying 'Informed' May Be," *American Coal*, Spring 2009. www.clean.coal.info.

Hendricks is communications director for the American Coal Ash Association.

❝'Clean' is not a word that normally leaps to mind for a commodity some spoilsports associate with unsafe mines, mountaintop removal, acid rain, black lung, lung cancer, asthma, mercury contamination, and, of course, global warming.❞

—Richard Conniff, "The Myth of Clean Coal," Environment 360, June 3, 2008. http://e360.yale.edu.

Conniff is an author and a recipient of the prestigious Guggenheim Fellowship.

❝Continuous improvements in technology have dramatically reduced or eliminated many of the environmental impacts traditionally associated with the use of coal in the vital electricity generation and steelmaking industries.❞

—World Coal Institute, "Coal & the Environment," 2009. www.worldcoal.org.

The World Coal Institute is an international organization representing the coal industry.

❝Coal use from cradle to the grave is dirty, dangerous, and damaging, and yet the coal industry is spending millions on lobbying to retain and create more loopholes for themselves.❞

—Mary Anne Hitt, "Coal Ash Sites Kept Secret, While Industry Works to Prevent Regulation," Sierra Club Compass blog, June 18, 2009. http://sierraclub.typepad.com.

Hitt is the deputy director of the Sierra Club's Beyond Coal Campaign.

❝Coal-fired plants release sulfur dioxides and nitrogen oxides, which are a primary cause of acid rain that harms trees and lakes and impairs visibility. . . . Air pollution from power plants can drift significant distances downwind and degrade air quality in nearby areas.❞

—U.S. Department of Justice, "Coal-Fired Power Plant to Spend More than $135 Million to Settle Clean Air Violations," news release, February 3, 2009. www.usdoj.gov.

The U.S. Department of Justice is the United States' primary law enforcement agency.

Facts and Illustrations

Does Coal Burning Threaten the Environment?

- According to the Sierra Club, coal-fired power plants emit nearly **60 percent** of the total U.S. sulfur dioxide pollution.

- Greenpeace states that pollution from coal-fired power plants causes **23,600** premature deaths, **21,850** hospital admissions, **554,000** asthma attacks, and **38,200** heart attacks every year.

- A study published in 2008 in the journal *Environmental Health Perspectives* reported that children born after the closure of a coal-burning plant in China had **60 percent** fewer developmental problems.

- According to a 2007 report by the U.S. Environmental Protection Agency, lagoons and landfills that are filled with coal combustion waste may present a cancer risk that is **10,000** times greater than federal regulatory rules allow.

- The Sierra Club states that every year **90 million gallons** (341 million L) of slurry (liquid waste) are produced while preparing coal to be burned, and **120 million tons** (109 million metric tons) of solid wastes are produced by burning coal.

Toxic Coal Waste and Cancer Risk

The Sierra Club states that coal-fired power plants produce an estimated 131 million tons (119 million metric tons) of waste every year. When it is disposed of in waste impoundments or landfills, toxins such as arsenic, mercury, and lead can leach into nearby soil and groundwater. In August 2007 the U.S. Environmental Protection Agency published a report showing that this contamination posed a high risk to human health. This graph shows the EPA's findings on the cancer risk from arsenic in coal ash compared with the risk from cigarette smoking.

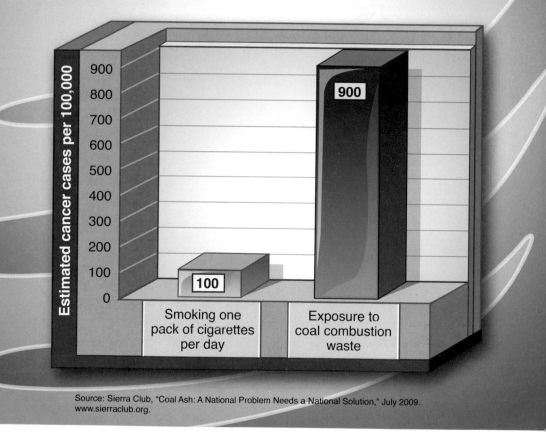

Source: Sierra Club, "Coal Ash: A National Problem Needs a National Solution," July 2009. www.sierraclub.org.

- The National Mining Association states that regulated emissions from coal-based electricity generation have decreased in the United States by nearly **40 percent** since the 1970s, while over that same time coal use has tripled.

Americans' Views About Energy Generation

As the world's reliance on coal for power plants and industry grows, environmental organizations warn that increased coal burning will be detrimental to the environment. Yet in an August 2009 poll by the *Washington Post* and ABC News, the majority of respondents either supported or strongly supported building more fossil fuel power plants, including coal-fired plants.

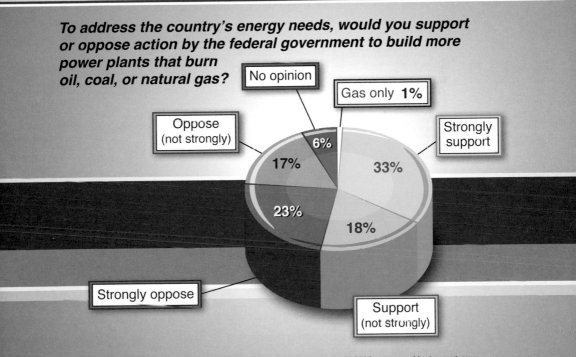

To address the country's energy needs, would you support or oppose action by the federal government to build more power plants that burn oil, coal, or natural gas?

No opinion

Gas only **1%**

Oppose (not strongly)

Strongly support

6%

17%

33%

23%

18%

Strongly oppose

Support (not strongly)

Source: *Washington Post*, "*Washington Post*-ABC News Poll," August 19, 2009. www.washingtonpost.com.

- A 2007 report by researchers at the Massachusetts Institute of Technology states that a 500-megawatt coal-fired power plant produces approximately **3 million tons** (2.7 million metric tons) of CO_2 per year and that the United States produces about **1.5 billion tons** (1.36 billion metric tons) of CO_2 from coal-burning power plants per year.

CO₂ Emissions from Power Plants

When fossil fuels are burned to generate electricity, they emit carbon dioxide into the atmosphere but emissions from coal-fired power plants contribute nearly five times more CO_2 than natural gas and oil combined. Many scientists warn that CO_2 buildup in the atmosphere is the biggest contributor to global warming.

CO₂ Emissions from Electricity Generation by Fuel

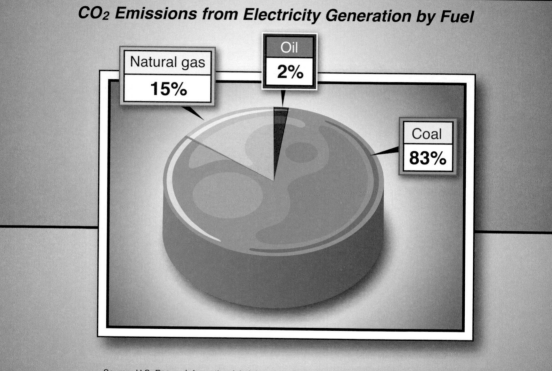

Natural gas
15%

Oil
2%

Coal
83%

Source: U.S. Energy Information Administration, *Greenhouse Gases, Climate Change & Energy,* May 2008. www.eia.doe.gov.

- According to a July 2007 report, the U.S. Environmental Protection Agency has identified more than **600 coal ash waste** sites in the United States, and the agency has found nearly 70 proven or potential cases of surface water or groundwater contamination from coal ash in at least 23 states.

What Are the Environmental Effects of Coal Mining?

66Coal mining can cause irreparable harm to the natural landscape, both during mining and after.99

—Alice McKeown, research associate at the Worldwatch Institute.

66Steps are taken in modern mining operations to minimise impacts on all aspects of the environment.99

—World Coal Institute, an international association representing the coal industry.

F or decades people living in coal-rich areas of the world have known about the environmental impact of coal mining. The process of retrieving coal from the ground takes a heavy toll on the land and water. Surface mining methods such as strip mining are often blamed for the worst damage, but underground mining also has adverse environmental effects. In Saarwellingen, Germany, for example, 300 years of underground mining was determined to be the cause of an earthquake in February 2008. According to a news article about the event, such quakes are caused when sandstone layers above mining holes break, which creates waves that make the ground above vibrate.

The Saarwellingen quake was the strongest ever recorded in the area, and the town sustained substantial damage. The shaking ground caused wide cracks in buildings, toppled chimneys, cut off electrical power, and pushed heavy blocks off the steeple of a church located near the mine.

Erika Ihiebert, whose chimney collapsed during the quake, shares her thoughts about the experience: "I thought I would die. It felt like the ceiling was going to come down on me." Like many residents, Ihiebert is frustrated and angry that the town's coal mine caused what is usually considered a natural disaster. "You see earthquakes on TV," she says. "That's bad enough, but at least, those are caused by nature. Ours are man-made. This must stop."[26] After acknowledging that mining operations were responsible for the earthquake, the owners permanently closed the mine.

Coal Mining Fills a Need

Coal mines feed the world's need for coal power, and that need is growing. Coal power is the predominant source of electricity in much of the world and is likely to be even more important in the coming years. For instance, countries such as China and South Korea plan to increase the number of coal-fired power plants.

Without adequate supplies of coal, many industries such as electricity generation and steel and cement manufacturing would suffer. For this reason, mining continues in about 70 countries, with the greatest mining activity in China, the United States, India, Australia, Russia, and South Africa. Mining operations in these countries supply much of the world's coal needs. Consequently, these countries also suffer the environmental effects that go along with being the world's largest coal suppliers.

Benefits Versus Costs

Appalachia has long been known as a coal-rich area, and mining has provided tens of thousands of people with jobs and steady incomes. But according to a study by researchers from West Virginia and Washington State universities, the costs associated with coal mining far outweigh the economic benefits. The report, entitled "Mortality in Appalachian Coal Mining Regions: The Value of Statistical Life Lost," was published in the July/August 2009 issue of the journal *Public Health Reports*. It shows that while the coal mining industry contributed about $8 billion to the economies of Appalachian states, the indirect costs of impaired human health and higher mortality rates associated with coal mining operations ranged from nearly $17 billion to $84.5 billion. This study and others before it have found that residents of coal-producing regions are more

likely to suffer from lung cancer and chronic diseases of the
heart, lung, and kidneys.

The researchers found that
areas of Appalachia where coal
is heavily mined had nearly
11,000 more deaths each year
than non-mining commu-
nities in the United States.
An estimated 2,300 of those
deaths were directly attribut-
able to air and water pollution
caused by coal mining. As the
report's authors write:

> According to a study
> by researchers from
> West Virginia and
> Washington State
> universities, the
> costs associated
> with coal mining far
> outweigh the eco-
> nomic benefits.

> Natural resources such as forests and streams have sub-
> stantial economic value when they are left intact, and
> mining is highly destructive of these resources. For exam-
> ple, Appalachian coal mining permanently buried 724
> stream miles between 1985 and 2001 through moun-
> taintop removal mining and subsequent valley fills, and
> will ultimately impact more than 1.4 million acres. Coal
> generates inexpensive electricity, but not as inexpensive
> as the price signals indicate because those prices do not
> include the costs to human health and productivity, and
> the costs of natural resource destruction.[27]

Effects of Coal Mining on Water Supplies

Jennifer Hall-Massey is well aware of the environmental impact of coal
mining. She and her family live in West Virginia, in the heart of Appalachian coal country. The mountains surrounding their home have long
been mined for coal, and for years no one living there experienced any
problems with pollution—but about a decade ago that changed. People
in the area began to notice that tap water smelled horrible and was often
cloudy, gray colored, and oily looking. Rust-colored rings showed up in
bathtubs, sinks, and washing machines, and no amount of effort could
scrub the stains away. Hall-Massey's husband installed water filters, and

they almost immediately turned black. When the Hall-Masseys' water was tested, it was found to contain exorbitantly high levels of lead, manganese, barium, and other toxic heavy metals—all of which are dangerous to human health.

The changes in the water, it was later discovered, were occurring about the same time that three nearby mining companies began injecting hundreds of millions of gallons of industrial waste into the ground or dumping it into lagoons. Eventually, toxins contained in the waste seeped into the groundwater. Three of those mining operations admitted that more than 90 percent of their waste sludge contained illegal concentrations of chemicals such as arsenic, lead, chromium, and nickel. According to a September 2009 article in the *New York Times*, toxic chemical concentrations sometimes exceeded legal limits by as much as 1,000 percent.

> According to the U.S. Geological Survey, drainage from thousands of abandoned coal mines in Pennsylvania has contaminated more than 3,000 miles (4,800km) of streams and groundwater throughout the state.

Hall-Massey's family has suffered because of this water pollution. Her six-year-old son, Clay, has rashes and scabs on his arms, legs, and chest from toxic metals contained in bathwater, and she must apply prescription ointment to ease the pain. Clay's older brother, Ryan, had to have crowns put on many of his teeth to replace enamel that had been eaten away by chemicals in the water that he used to brush his teeth.

Other people in the community have had similar or worse experiences. According to the *Times* article, in addition to rashes and chemical burns on the skin, residents have suffered serious health problems such as gall bladder disease, infertility, miscarriages, and illnesses affecting the kidneys and thyroid. Ben Stout, a biology professor at Wheeling Jesuit University, tested the water in Hall-Massey's community as well as other areas of West Virginia, and he says there is no doubt that the mining companies are responsible: "I don't know what else could be polluting these wells. The chemicals coming out of people's taps are identical to the chemicals the coal companies are pumping into the ground."[28]

Acid Mine Drainage

Nearly three-fourths of the coal in the United States is mined using surface mining methods such as strip mining. After workers have removed the overburden so they can reach the coal seams, tons of rock and soil are cast aside as waste. When the overburden is exposed to air and water, pyrite, a mineral that is found in rocks that contain coal, undergoes a chemical change and forms sulfuric acid. As rainwater washes over the rocks, the runoff becomes acidified, a phenomenon known as acid mine drainage. When the runoff reaches soil, rivers, and streams, the effect is similar to what happens with acid rain.

Acid mine drainage also occurs when abandoned underground coal mines fill with water. According to the U.S. Geological Survey, drainage from thousands of abandoned coal mines in Pennsylvania has contaminated more than 3,000 miles (4,800km) of streams and groundwater throughout the state. This, says the agency, "is the most extensive water-pollution problem affecting the four major river basins in Pennsylvania."[29] Toxic concentrations of acids, metals, and sediment have killed most of the fish in these streams.

> " Three of those mining operations admitted that more than 90 percent of their waste sludge contained illegal concentrations of chemicals such as arsenic, lead, chromium, and nickel. "

Disappearing Mountains

As coal supplies have become more difficult to reach, mining companies have increasingly turned to mountaintop removal mining. This method involves using explosives to blast off the tops of mountains so workers can more easily reach the deeply buried coal. In the process, thousands of acres of trees in ancient forests are cut down to clear the land. Millions of tons of rock and other overburden are bulldozed out of the ground and either piled in massive heaps or dumped into valleys and streams. According to the Sierra Club and other environmental organizations, mountaintop removal mining is the most environmentally devastating method of retrieving coal from the earth.

Science and environmental journalist John McQuaid says that mountaintop removal mining destroys forests and streams, fouls waterways farther down the mountain, and permanently disrupts delicate forest ecology. He writes:

> The Appalachian Mountain range dates back 300 million years. Its coal is the residue of peat bogs formed in tropical coastal swamps when there was a single supercontinent, Pangaea. But it takes only a matter of months to tear down a mountain peak using explosives and giant excavators. . . . Since the mid-1990s, the coal industry has cut a swath of devastation through Appalachia's remote, coal-rich highlands, one of the nation's most dramatic cases of environmental devastation and regulatory failure.[30]

McQuaid refers also to a study by the U.S. Environmental Protection Agency that estimates that by 2012 mountaintop removal projects in Appalachia will have destroyed or seriously damaged more than 1 million acres (405,000ha) of forest—an area larger than the state of Delaware—and buried over 1,000 miles (1,610km) of mountain streams.

Land Reclamation

In accordance with the 1977 Surface Mining Control and Reclamation Act, once coal mines are no longer in use, mining operations are required by law to restore mine sites as close as possible to the way they were prior to the mines being built. The legislation refers to this as approximate original contour, or AOC. Once coal supplies have been exhausted, mining companies must repair the land by building wetlands and planting trees and other vegetation. As the American Coal Foundation explains: "In the past, coal mining often left behind landscapes that were unattractive and unproductive. Animals and plant life that once thrived in an area could no longer survive in conditions produced by coal mining. Today, thanks to land reclamation, it can be difficult to tell the difference between land that has been mined and land that has not."[31] The National

Mining Association states that since 1978 more than 2.2 million acres (890,000ha) of mined lands have been restored to their original condition or better.

Many environmentalists disagree that mining companies are repairing the land. Research has shown that these companies are not always in compliance with the law and instead leave the land irreparably scarred by mountaintop removal and other strip mining processes. This was the focus of a study announced in July 2009 by the Office of Surface Mining, which examined retired strip mines in southern West Virginia. Investigators found that mine operators were not repairing the land in compliance with their mining permits. According to Joe Lovett, director of the Appalachian Center for the Economy and the Environment, post-mining development of mountaintop removal sites is rare in the region. Mountains and valleys that have "changed dramatically in contour" are unstable for development and no longer support native vegetation, says Lovett. He adds:

> If mines are restored to AOC the disturbed area is smaller, valley fills and stream impacts are reduced. Remarkably, there are few, if any, large surface mines in Appalachia that comply with this basic requirement. Instead, mining operators . . . thumb their noses at the law and create monstrous valley fills and sawed off mountains that more closely resemble the surface of the moon than our lush, green hills.[32]

Can This Be Resolved?

Although coal power is invaluable for electricity generation and manufacturing, the issue of coal mining is controversial. Mine operations provide jobs to thousands of people, yet research casts doubt on whether the economic benefits outweigh the cost to human health. Organizations such as the American Coal Foundation say their members go out of their way to return the land to its natural state after strip mines are no longer used, but that has also been questioned. So is there a solution to this dilemma? With such radically differing viewpoints about coal mining's effects on the environment, that question is not likely to be answered for a very long time—if ever.

What Are the Environmental Effects of Coal Mining?

> **Above ground, millions of acres across 36 states have been dynamited, torn and churned into bits by strip mining in the last 150 years.**

—Jeff Biggers, "'Clean' Coal? Don't Try to Shovel That," *Washington Post*, March 2, 2008. www.washingtonpost.com.

Biggers is the author of *The United States of Appalachia: How Southern Mountaineers Brought Independence, Culture and Enlightenment to America.*

....

> **For many years people have only heard the voice of those opposing coal mining. It is time for the world to see that there is a brighter side to coal mining.**

—Coal Mining Our Future, "Before During & After," 2009. www.coalminingourfuture.net.

Coal Mining Our Future is an organization of southeastern Kentucky coal mining companies.

....

Bracketed quotes indicate conflicting positions.

* Editor's Note: While the definition of a primary source can be narrowly or broadly defined, for the purposes of Compact Research, a primary source consists of: 1) results of original research presented by an organization or researcher; 2) eyewitness accounts of events, personal experience, or work experience; 3) first-person editorials offering pundits' opinions; 4) government officials presenting political plans and/or policies; 5) representatives of organizations presenting testimony or policy.

66Surface mining, including open pit or strip mining, is less dangerous than underground mining, but has a greater impact on surface landscapes.**99**

—Environmental Literacy Council, "Coal Mining," June 26, 2008. www.enviroliteracy.org.

The Environmental Literacy Council works with educators in the teaching of environmental science.

66Mountaintop removal, which provides a mere 7 percent of the nation's coal, is done by clear-cutting forests, blowing the tops off of mountains, and then dumping the debris into streambeds—an undeniably catastrophic way of mining.**99**

—James Hansen, "A Plea to President Obama: End Mountaintop Coal Mining," Environment 360, June 22, 2009. http://e360.yale.edu.

Hansen is the director of NASA's Goddard Institute for Space Studies and an adjunct professor in the Department of Earth and Environmental Sciences at Columbia University.

66Mountaintop mining is simply coal mining that occurs at or near the topmost portion of a mountain. There have been various emotional statements in the press about this form of mining that are neither based on fact nor supported by the truth.**99**

—Coalition for Mountaintop Mining, "What Is Mountaintop Mining?" 2009. http://mrmcoalition.com.

The Coalition for Mountaintop Mining provides information about the coal industry and the practice of mountaintop mining.

66Why do we surface mine in Central Appalachia? . . . The fundamental answer is that coal is surface mined because that is the method necessary to recover the resource.**99**

—Gene Kitts, "Why Surface Mine?" Coal Mining Our Future, July 27, 2009. www.coalminingourfuture.net.

Kitts is senior vice president of mining services for the International Coal Group.

66 Coal companies may not love mountains but they sure love to tout how they restore mountaintops after they remove them by blasting, digging and dumping. 99

—Rob Perks, "Mountaintop Removal: FAIL," *Huffington Post*, August 25, 2009. www.huffingtonpost.com.

Perks is the director of the Natural Resources Defense Council's Center for Advocacy Campaigns.

66 Mining companies are constantly seeking better methods of reclaiming mined lands. 99

—National Mining Association, "Reclamation," 2009. www.nma.org.

The National Mining Association represents the American coal-mining industry.

What Are the Environmental Effects of Coal Mining?

- According to a September 2009 report by the Energy Information Administration, the United States has **1,458 operating coal mines**, 1,351 of which are located east of the Mississippi River.

- The National Mining Association states that about **70 percent** of the coal in the United States is mined using surface mining methods such as strip mining and mountaintop removal mining.

- The Energy Information Administration states that between 1949 and 2008 the number of surface mines in the United States grew from 122 to **852**.

- A ton (0.9 metric tons) of coal can be extracted through strip mining methods at barely **one-fifth** the cost of underground mining.

- The Environmental Literacy Council states that for every ton of coal that is mined, approximately **25 tons (23 metric tons) of topsoil**, or overburden, is removed from the ground, which can lead to erosion, loss of wildlife habitat, and dust pollution.

- Every day, coal mining processes require as much as **260 million gallons** (984 million L) of water.

The Growth of Surface Mines

The growing worldwide demand for energy requires a steady source of coal that can be retrieved economically. Underground mining is the cheapest method as well as the least harmful to the environment. But because U.S. coal is often buried too deep to reach economically, an estimated 70 percent is retrieved through surface mining methods, which are considered more harmful to the environment. Between 1949 and 2008 the number of surface mines in the United States rose from 122 to 852–an increase of nearly 600 percent.

Surface Mines in the United States—1949 to 2008

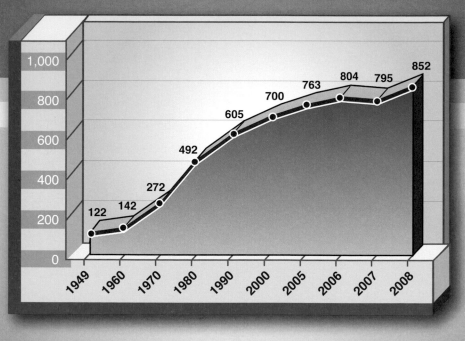

Sources: U.S. Energy Information Administration, *Annual Energy Review 2008,* June 2009. www.eia.doe.gov; U.S. Energy Information Administration, *Annual Coal Report 2008*, September 18, 2009. www.eia.doe.gov.

- The estimated cost of restoring Pennsylvania watersheds damaged by mining is **$5 billion to $15 billion**, according to the U.S. Geological Survey.

People Say No to Mountaintop Removal Mining

To meet the growing demand for coal, mining companies in Appalachia use mountaintop removal mining, which allows them to reach deeply buried coal reserves. This method is considered environmentally destructive and has little public support, according to a 2008 opinion poll in which the majority of participants expressed opposition after hearing a description of mountaintop removal mining.

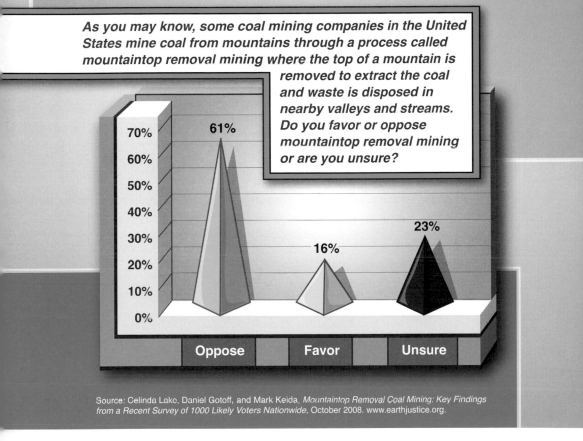

As you may know, some coal mining companies in the United States mine coal from mountains through a process called mountaintop removal mining where the top of a mountain is removed to extract the coal and waste is disposed in nearby valleys and streams. Do you favor or oppose mountaintop removal mining or are you unsure?

- Oppose: 61%
- Favor: 16%
- Unsure: 23%

Source: Celinda Lako, Daniel Gotoff, and Mark Keida, *Mountaintop Removal Coal Mining: Key Findings from a Recent Survey of 1000 Likely Voters Nationwide*, October 2008. www.earthjustice.org.

- According to the Web site iLoveMountains, nearly **500 mountains** in the United States have been destroyed by mountaintop removal mining.

The Decapitation of Mountains

Of all the types of coal mining that exist, mountaintop removal mining has been called the most destructive because mountains are literally blasted apart, with the overburden (waste material) dumped into valleys and streams. This process destroys the ecosystem that existed there before mining began. This illustration shows how the process works from beginning to end.

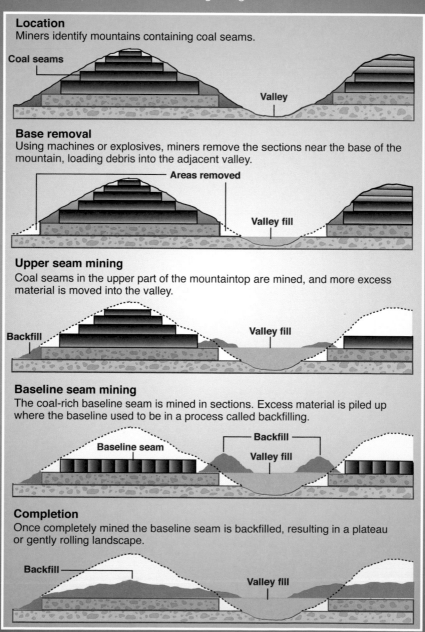

Location
Miners identify mountains containing coal seams.

Coal seams

Valley

Base removal
Using machines or explosives, miners remove the sections near the base of the mountain, loading debris into the adjacent valley.

Areas removed

Valley fill

Upper seam mining
Coal seams in the upper part of the mountaintop are mined, and more excess material is moved into the valley.

Backfill

Valley fill

Baseline seam mining
The coal-rich baseline seam is mined in sections. Excess material is piled up where the baseline used to be in a process called backfilling.

Backfill

Baseline seam

Valley fill

Completion
Once completely mined the baseline seam is backfilled, resulting in a plateau or gently rolling landscape.

Backfill

Valley fill

Source: Tom Hamburder and Peter Wallsten, "A Quiet OK for Peak's Removal," *Los Angeles Times,* May 31, 2009. www.latimes.com.

- A study announced in March 2008 by researchers at West Virginia University showed that people who live in coal mining communities have a **70 percent** increased risk for developing kidney disease and a **64 percent** increased risk for developing cardiopulmonary diseases such as emphysema.

- The National Mining Association states that since 1978, U.S. mining companies have paid more than **$7 billion** to reclaim mines that were abandoned prior to laws requiring reclamation.

- According to the Union of Concerned Scientists, more than **300,000 acres** (121,000ha) of hardwood forests and **1,000 miles** (1,610km) of streams in West Virginia have been destroyed by surface mining.

- Researchers at West Virginia University announced in 2008 that mortality data for West Virginia suggests there are **313 excess deaths** every year from coal mining pollution.

- The U.S. Bureau of Land Management states that as of April 2008 there were more than **12,000 abandoned mines** on public lands in the United States, and only about **20 percent** have been restored to their previous state and cleansed of harmful residues or have reclamation actions planned.

What Is the Future of Coal Power?

66If America doesn't seriously begin the transition to renewable energy now, we may well get caught, not many years hence, with too little coal and not enough installed alternatives.99

—Richard Heinberg, senior fellow of the Post Carbon Institute.

66Coal is cheap and plentiful, and the United States is going to use it for the foreseeable future. Even if we did not, China and India would, so rapid development and deployment of climate-friendly technologies is essential.99

—Eileen Claussen, president of the Pew Center on Global Climate Change.

As one of the world's most polluted countries, China may seem an unlikely leader in the advancement of clean coal technologies—yet it is definitely heading that way. Over the past two years (2008–2010), as China has constructed an average of one to two new coal-fired power plants each week, the country has focused on building facilities that are more efficient and less polluting than older plants. The government has also mandated that energy companies retire one older, high-polluting power plant for each new plant that they build. "The steps they've taken are probably as fast and as serious as anywhere in power-generation history,"[33] says Hal Harvey, president of the environmental financing group ClimateWorks.

One way that China has reduced its emissions of CO_2 and polluting gases such as sulfur dioxide is by embracing supercritical technology, in which coal is burned at extremely high temperatures to create superheated steam. This raises the plant's efficiency to more than 44 percent, compared with the worldwide average of 31 percent for coal-fired plants that lack such technology. Currently, China has more than 20 supercritical power plants in operation, including 4 that feature ultra-supercritical technology, which is even more sophisticated. These power plants achieve nearly 50 percent efficiency and emit far fewer pollutants into the atmosphere than any other type of coal-fired power plant. According to a 2009 report by the International Energy Agency, China has emerged as a world leader in the development of cleaner, more efficient coal-burning technologies, and the country will likely continue this leadership position in the future.

> " Over the past two years (2008–2010), as China has constructed an average of one to two new coal-fired power plants each week, the country has focused on building facilities that are more efficient and less polluting than older plants. "

Cleaning Up Coal

Because coal is known for being the dirtiest of all fossil fuels, organizations such as the American Coalition for Clean Coal Electricity support the development of technologies that make coal burn more cleanly. One particularly avid supporter is Gregory Boyce, who is chair of the coal company Peabody Energy. "Technologies are changing the color of coal," he writes, "ultimately enabling us to achieve the goal of near-zero emissions. I like to say that black is the new green." Boyce adds that clean coal has a long record of success, and this will continue in the coming years. He says:

Major technology investments have significantly reduced emissions over the past several decades. As coal used for electricity generation has tripled since 1970, coal's environmental efficiency has dramatically improved, resulting in an 84 percent reduction of regulated emissions per ton of coal. In the past 20 years alone, America's electric utilities have invested nearly $100 billion in clean coal technologies.[34]

Critics of coal power dispute the term "clean coal," arguing that coal power is not and never will be clean. They point out that even though coal-fired power plants are required to install scrubbers to remove pollutants before emissions go into the air, CO_2 is not regulated, and scrubbers do not remove it. Thus, coal-fired plants throughout the world continue to emit billions of tons of CO_2 into the atmosphere every year. David Roberts, a senior writer for the environmental blog Grist, shares his views: "Not a single commercial coal power plant in America captures or otherwise prevents CO_2 emissions. 'Clean coal' is a PR gimmick."[35]

Gasification Technology

Since coal is such an important fuel worldwide, especially for electricity generation, scientists project that it will continue to be burned for decades to come. This is a concern mainly because CO_2 accumulation in the atmosphere is believed to contribute to global warming. That is why a type of technology known as gasification is so promising, as the U.S. Department of Energy explains: "Coal gasification offers one of the most versatile and clean ways to convert coal into electricity, hydrogen, and other valuable energy products. Coal gasification electric power plants are now operating commercially in the United States and in other nations, and many experts predict that coal gasification will be at the heart of future generations of clean coal technology plants."[36]

Unlike traditional power plants that burn coal to generate steam, gasification plants use a thermochemical process to "gasify" coal, or break it down into its basic chemical properties. Under very high temperatures and pressures, gasifiers expose coal to steam and controlled amounts of air or oxygen. This causes the molecules in coal to split apart, which initiates chemical reactions that typically produce a mixture of carbon monoxide, hydrogen, and other gaseous substances. When coal is gasified in this way, the process removes sulfur dioxide, mercury, and CO_2 from the synthetic gas (known as syngas) before it is combusted, making the fuel much cleaner than raw coal.

One syngas plant is located near Beulah, North Dakota, and has been in operation since 1988. The Great Plains Synfuels Plant is the only commercial-scale plant in the United States that manufactures natural gas by gasifying coal. Every day, the plant produces an estimated 145 million cubic feet (4.1 million cubic m) of natural gas, most of which is sent via pipeline to Ventura, Iowa, for distribution in the eastern United States. The Synfuels Plant also uses the gas it produces to manufacture other products such as ammonium sulfate and anhydrous ammonia, which are used as agricultural fertilizers; liquid nitrogen, which is used for refrigeration by food processing operations; and krypton and xenon gases, used for specialty lighting as well as thermopane window insulation.

> " Since coal is such an important fuel worldwide, especially for electricity generation, scientists project that it will continue to be burned for decades to come. "

Capturing and Storing Carbon

A number of scientists are excited about a kind of technology known as carbon capture and sequestration (CCS) because of its vast potential to reduce CO_2 in the atmosphere. According to the International Energy Agency, CCS has the ability to reduce CO_2 emissions from coal-fired power plants by more than 85 percent. The process is the same as is used by gasification plants, but instead of creating new types of fuel, the CO_2 is captured, compressed to a near-liquid state, and transported via pipeline to various locations. For instance, the Antelope Valley Station in North Dakota captures more than 1 million tons (907,200 metric tons) of CO_2 each year and pipes it 205 miles (330km) away to Dakota Gas in Saskatchewan, Canada. Dakota uses the CO_2 for enhanced oil recovery, a process that enables higher yields of oil to be recovered from the earth.

Workers pump the CO_2 at high pressure into 37 injection wells, where it mixes with the oil and expands. This forces the oil out of pores in the rocks so it can flow more easily toward producer wells that pump it out of the ground.

The *sequestration* part of CCS refers to CO_2 that is compressed and then piped deep into the earth where it is stored, or sequestered, for safe-keeping. According to the Web site Carbon Capture & Sequestration, oil and gas have been stored under layers of impermeable cap rock for millions of years. "As the oil and gas is produced," the Web site reports, "it travels through the porous rock to a well and then to the surface, essentially freeing space between the grains of rock where CO_2 can be injected to replace the produced oil and gas."[37] A highly successful CCS facility is the Sleipner gas field, which is located in the North Sea off the coast of Norway. Operational since 1996, it is the oldest industrial-scale CCS project in the world. Since the facility opened, more than 11 million tons (10 million metric tons) of CO_2 have been injected into layers of sandstone 3,300 feet (1,000m) below the seafloor.

> **When coal is gasified . . . the process removes sulfur dioxide, mercury, and CO_2 from the synthetic gas (known as syngas) before it is combusted, making the fuel much cleaner than raw coal.**

As excited as many scientists are about CCS technology, it also has its detractors. Emily Rochon, who is a climate and energy campaigner for Greenpeace, says that the focus should not be on how to store CO_2, but rather on how to wean the world from coal. "We need to pick our future," she says. "Do we want a green energy future or do we want a black energy future?" Rochon adds that CCS is not the answer to global energy challenges. "It keeps fossil-intensive energy infrastructure in place and at the top of the energy agenda. We've never given renewable energy the chance it deserves, so it hasn't taken off."[38] There are other challenges with CCS as well, one of which is the expense. The U.S. Department of Energy estimates that installing CCS systems would nearly double the cost of building coal-fired power plants, and this would inevitably lead to steep hikes in the cost of electricity.

Another concern that many people have with CCS is the potential risks of pumping extraordinary amounts of CO_2 into the ground or seafloor. They fear that the gas could leak, which could put humans at risk as well as destroy wildlife and marine ecosystems. There is no record of this sort of thing happening, and there has never been a leak at the Sleipner facility. But a natural disaster that occurred in 1986 is often used as a warning by those who are concerned about long-term storage of CO_2. In Cameroon, which is located in western Africa, is a lake named Lake Nyos. It is an unusual geologic phenomenon because it formed hundreds of years ago when a volcano erupted and filled with water. Afterward, a magma chamber that had been feeding the volcano began to release CO_2 into the bottom of the lake, where the gas slowly accumulated under pressure.

> "
> A number of scientists are excited about a kind of technology known as carbon capture and sequestration (CCS) because of its vast potential to reduce CO_2 in the atmosphere.
> "

On the evening of August 21, 1986, residents of Nyos felt the earth rumbling and then heard a deafening boom coming from the lake. Suddenly, the stored CO_2 burst through the surface of the water and blasted high into the air, leaving catastrophe in its wake. CBC News explains:

> The invisible gas, heavier than air, roared through the valley, displacing oxygen and suffocating every living creature—1,800 people, 3,000 cattle and countless birds and insects—in a death zone that spread 19 kilometres. Residents who heard the boom and went to their doorways died where they stood. Others who were standing survived, while family members lying down beside them, closer to the floor, never woke up.[39]

Those who are most concerned about the potential risks of CCS say that storing vast amounts of CO_2 beneath the earth could potentially result in the same sort of disaster.

Changing Coal into Baking Soda?

Joe David Jones has a dream that he is passionate about. The founder and CEO of a company called Skyonic, he has developed an industrial process whereby 90 percent of the CO_2 emitted by smokestacks can be captured, cleaned, and recycled into sodium bicarbonate—better known as baking soda. The technology, known as SkyMine, is designed to work with any large-scale industry, including power plants that are fired by coal, oil, or natural gas. The process involves capturing flue emissions and removing heavy metals such as mercury, sulfur dioxide, and nitrogen oxide, which are stored for later disposal. Once the CO_2 has been isolated, it is mixed with sodium hydroxide (also known as caustic soda), which causes chemical changes to take place. The result is sodium bicarbonate—an exorbitant amount of it.

> Skyonic is convinced that SkyMine could replace coal scrubbers, which would not only eliminate millions of dollars in annual operating costs, but also keep billions of tons of CO_2 out of the atmosphere.

Because of the sheer volume of the substance that would be created if all factories converted CO_2 into baking soda, its uses would obviously not be limited to baking or keeping the refrigerator smelling fresh. But there are many other potential uses as well, such as filling in coal mines or being recycled for use in industrial operations. Even if the baking soda were dumped in landfills, it would not pollute the air, soil, or groundwater. Also, SkyMine's cost of an estimated $400 million is about the same cost of scrubbers that power plants must install in order to be in compliance with environmental laws. Skyonic is convinced that SkyMine could replace coal scrubbers, which would not only eliminate millions of dollars in costs for operating them, but also keep billions of tons of CO_2 out of the atmosphere.

Looking Ahead

Although coal is a finite resource that will eventually be depleted, it will likely remain one of the world's most important fuels for decades to come. But because of its environmental impact, scientists are exploring ways to make coal burn more cleanly, as well as developing methods of capturing CO_2 and either using it to create other products or sequestering it deep beneath the surface of the earth. As more sophisticated technologies continue to be developed, coal may someday cease to be known as the dirtiest of all fuels. Whether that will ever happen, however, remains unknown.

What Is the Future of Coal Power?

66 **Clean coal: Never was there an oxymoron more insidious, or more dangerous to our public health.** 99

—Jeff Biggers, "'Clean' Coal? Don't Try to Shovel That," *Washington Post*, March 2, 2008. www.washingtonpost.com.

Biggers is the author of *The United States of Appalachia: How Southern Mountaineers Brought Independence, Culture and Enlightenment to America.*

66 **Clean coal is the ultimate solution for re-energizing the U.S. and world economies, creating millions of green jobs and building long-term, sustainable energy security. In recent years, clean coal has been a tremendous success story.** 99

—Stephan Miller, "Clean Coal, Progress, and the Classics," *American Coal*, Spring 2009. www.clean-coal.info.

Miller is president of the American Coal Council.

Bracketed quotes indicate conflicting positions.

* Editor's Note: While the definition of a primary source can be narrowly or broadly defined, for the purposes of Compact Research, a primary source consists of: 1) results of original research presented by an organization or researcher; 2) eyewitness accounts of events, personal experience, or work experience; 3) first-person editorials offering pundits' opinions; 4) government officials presenting political plans and/or policies; 5) representatives of organizations presenting testimony or policy.

❝Unfortunately, coal will be with us for some time to come. Even if the United States turns clean power into a top priority, it will take decades to wean ourselves off a fossil fuel that generates about half of our electricity.❞

—*Los Angeles Times*, "Coal Ash—a Tennessee Wake-Up Call," editorial, January 6, 2009. www.latimes.com.

The *Los Angeles Times* is the second-largest metropolitan newspaper in the United States.

❝Our data confirms that the world has enough proved reserves of oil, natural gas and coal to meet the world's needs for decades to come.❞

—Tony Hayward, "Energy in 2008 Followed the Economic Headlines," *BP Statistical Review of World Energy*, June 2009. www.bp.com.

Hayward is the group chief executive of British Petroleum, one of the world's largest energy companies.

❝It is not possible to confirm that there is a sufficient supply of coal for the next 250 years, as is often asserted.❞

—National Academy of Sciences, *Coal: Research and Development to Support National Energy Policy*, July 2007. http://books.nap.edu.

The National Academy of Sciences brings together experts in all areas of scientific and technological endeavor.

❝Coal is an abundant domestic energy resource. At current rates of consumption, coal could meet U.S. needs for more than 250 years.❞

—National Energy Technology Laboratory, "Technologies: Coal and Power Systems," 2009. www.netl.doe.gov.

An agency of the U.S. Department of Energy, the National Energy Technology Laboratory works to advance the national, economic, and energy security of the United States.

> ❝If we are going to end the recession, retain American jobs and living standards, and rejuvenate our economy, we will need vast quantities of electricity from coal—and every other energy source—now and for decades to come.❞

—Paul Driessen, "Coal Power Saves Lives," *American Coal*, Spring 2009. www.clean coal.info.

Driessen is senior policy advisor for the Congress of Racial Equality and the Committee for a Constructive Tomorrow.

> ❝The global demand for coal is now greater than ever before and it is expected to be a dominant energy source well into the foreseeable future. In fact, by 2100, it is projected that nearly half of the world's energy will come from coal.❞

—Judy Tanselle, "Realizing a Cleaner Coal," *American Coal*, Spring 2009. www.clean-coal.info.

Tanselle is the president of White Energy Coal North America.

> ❝All sources of energy will be needed to meet future energy demand, including coal.❞

—World Coal Institute, "Uses of Coal," 2009. www.worldcoal.org.

The World Coal Institute is an international association representing the coal industry.

> ❝Realistically, we need to recognize that we have trillions of dollars already invested in coal-based electrical plants and it is illogical to trash this, as it is also logistically impossible to replace it—with anything—in the medium term.❞

—Victor Rudolph, "Let's Be Realistic About Coal," *Seed*, July 2, 2009. http://seedmagazine.com.

Rudolph is a professor of chemical engineering at the University of Queensland in Australia.

What Is the Future of Coal Power?

- The World Coal Institute estimates that coal use will rise **60 percent** over the next 20 years.

- The Energy Information Administration projects that China's coal use for electricity generation will grow by **4.2 percent** each year through 2025.

- According to the Energy Information Administration, **steel manufacturing in Brazil** will more than double by 2018, which means the country will need to import increasing amounts of coal from the United States and other coal-rich countries.

- In 2007 the *Christian Science Monitor* reported that countries throughout the world will add enough coal-fired capacity in the next 5 years to send an extra **1.2 billion tons (1.09 billion metric tons) of CO_2** into the atmosphere each year.

- The World Coal Institute states that there is enough coal remaining worldwide to last about **130 years**.

- According to the group Alaska Coal, commercial-scale **carbon capture and sequestration projects** are not expected to be deployed in the United States until 2030.

- The Energy Information Administration projects that electricity demand in the United States will increase **41 percent** by 2030.

Global Coal Production in the Future

A May 2009 report by the U.S. Energy Information Administration predicts that coal production will continue to rise between now and 2030, most notably in China because of its heavy reliance on coal to power its growing industry. This graph shows the projections for six countries that are expected to have the largest increases in coal production.

World Coal Production Outlook—2010 to 2030

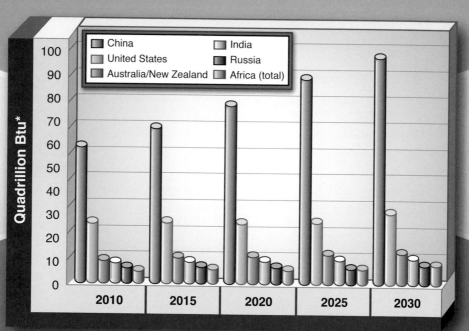

*British thermal unit (Btu) is a unit of energy used in the power, steam-generation, heating, and air-conditioning industries.

Source: U.S. Energy Information Administration, *International Energy Outlook: 2009*, May 2009. www.eia.doe.gov.

- A May 2007 report by National Public Radio stated that China will build **500 coal-fired power plants** in the next decade, at the rate of almost one per week.

Global View of Fossil Fuel–Fired Power Plants

To satisfy the world's demand for coal, a number of countries plan to increase the number of coal-fired power plants in operation over the coming decades. In a July–November 2008 poll by WorldPublicOpinion.org, 21,000 people from around the world were asked to share their thoughts about what energy sources should be used in the future. This graph shows how participants responded when asked about power plants fired by fossil fuels.

Question: *Should your country put more emphasis, less emphasis, or the same emphasis as now, on building coal- and oil-fired power plants?*

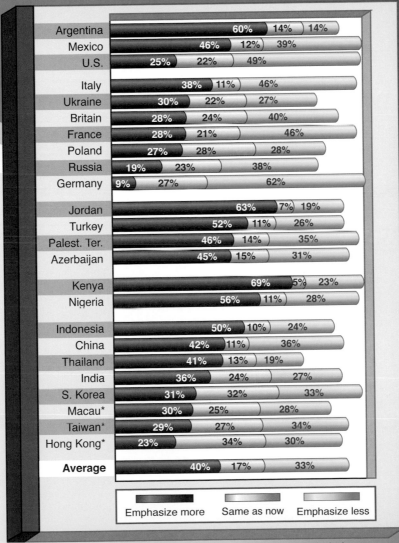

Country	Emphasize more	Same as now	Emphasize less
Argentina	60%	14%	14%
Mexico	46%	12%	39%
U.S.	25%	22%	49%
Italy	38%	11%	46%
Ukraine	30%	22%	27%
Britain	28%	24%	40%
France	28%	21%	46%
Poland	27%	28%	28%
Russia	19%	23%	38%
Germany	9%	27%	62%
Jordan	63%	7%	19%
Turkey	52%	11%	26%
Palest. Ter.	46%	14%	35%
Azerbaijan	45%	15%	31%
Kenya	69%	5%	23%
Nigeria	56%	11%	28%
Indonesia	50%	10%	24%
China	42%	11%	36%
Thailand	41%	13%	19%
India	36%	24%	27%
S. Korea	31%	32%	33%
Macau*	30%	25%	28%
Taiwan*	29%	27%	34%
Hong Kong*	23%	34%	30%
Average	40%	17%	33%

Note: Percents for "don't know/not sure" responses are not included.
* Not included in average

Source: WorldPublicOpinion.org, "World Publics Strongly Favor Requiring More Wind and Solar Energy, More Efficiency, Even If It Increases Costs," November 19, 2008. www.worldpublicopinion.org.

How Carbon Is Captured and Stored

With worldwide coal use continuing to rise, and concerns about carbon dioxide emissions growing, scientists are faced with the challenge of finding viable solutions that fill energy needs while not harming the environment. Many are excited about carbon capture and sequestration (CCS), which involves capturing carbon when it is emitted from smokestacks, turning it into a near-liquid form, and piping it deep within the earth where it is sequestered, or stored, for safekeeping. This illustration shows how CCS works.

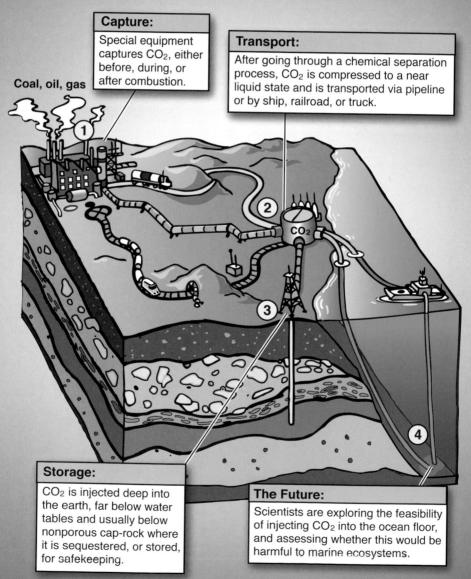

Capture:
Special equipment captures CO_2, either before, during, or after combustion.

Coal, oil, gas

Transport:
After going through a chemical separation process, CO_2 is compressed to a near liquid state and is transported via pipeline or by ship, railroad, or truck.

Storage:
CO_2 is injected deep into the earth, far below water tables and usually below nonporous cap-rock where it is sequestered, or stored, for safekeeping.

The Future:
Scientists are exploring the feasibility of injecting CO_2 into the ocean floor, and assessing whether this would be harmful to marine ecosystems.

Sources: Carbon Capture & Sequestration, "Frequently Asked Questions," www.ccs-education.net; Emily Rochon, *False Hope: Why Carbon Capture and Storage Won't Save the Climate*, May 2008. www.greenpeace.org.

U.S. Emission Pollutants Projected to Decline by 2030

According to the U.S. Energy Information Administration, even though coal will continue to play a major role in the generation of electricity, sulfur dioxide and nitrogen oxide pollution will decrease by 2030. Clean-coal technologies and reduced dependence on high-sulfur (soft) coal will contribute to the decrease.

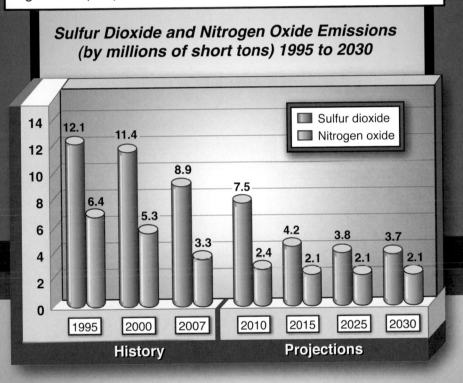

Sulfur Dioxide and Nitrogen Oxide Emissions (by millions of short tons) 1995 to 2030

Source: U.S. Energy Information Administration, *Annual Energy Outlook 2009—with Projections to 2030*, March 2009. www.eia.doe.

- A 2007 report by researchers from the Massachusetts Institute of Technology states that if **60 percent** of the CO_2 produced from U.S. coal-fired power generation were to be captured and compressed to a liquid (known as sequestration), its volume would equal the total U.S. oil consumption of **20 million barrels** per day.

Key People and Advocacy Groups

American Coal Council: A coal industry organization that is dedicated to advancing the development and utilization of coal as an economic, abundant, secure, and environmentally sound energy fuel source.

American Coal Foundation: A coal industry organization that develops, produces, and disseminates informative coal-related materials and programs designed for teachers and students.

American Coalition for Clean Coal Electricity: An organization dedicated to advancing the development and deployment of advanced clean coal technologies that will produce electricity with near-zero emissions.

Jeff Biggers: The grandson of a coal miner from southern Illinois, Biggers is the author of *The United States of Appalachia: How Southern Mountaineers Brought Independence, Culture and Enlightenment to America* and an outspoken critic of mountaintop removal mining in Appalachia.

Greenpeace: An activist organization that works to expose environmental problems throughout the world (including those that are caused by coal mining and coal burning) and proposes solutions that help solve those problems.

James Hansen: The director of NASA's Goddard Institute for Space Studies and an adjunct professor in the Department of Earth and Environmental Sciences at Columbia University, Hansen is an outspoken critic of coal power and its impact on the environment.

National Mining Association: A trade organization that represents the American mining industry before Congress, the administration, federal agencies, the judiciary, and the media.

Bruce Nilles: As director of the Sierra Club's Beyond Coal Campaign, Nilles works to ensure that the coal industry is accountable for environmental harm from coal mining and coal burning.

Sierra Club: A grassroots environmental movement that opposes the proliferation of coal power because of its effect on the land, air, and water.

Union of Concerned Scientists: A science-based nonprofit organization that works toward a healthy environment and a safer world.

U.S. Department of Energy Office of Fossil Energy: An agency whose primary mission is to ensure that the United States can continue to rely on clean, affordable energy from traditional fuel resources.

World Coal Institute: A United Kingdom–based organization that seeks to provide a forum for the exchange of information and the discussion of challenges relating to the coal industry.

Chronology

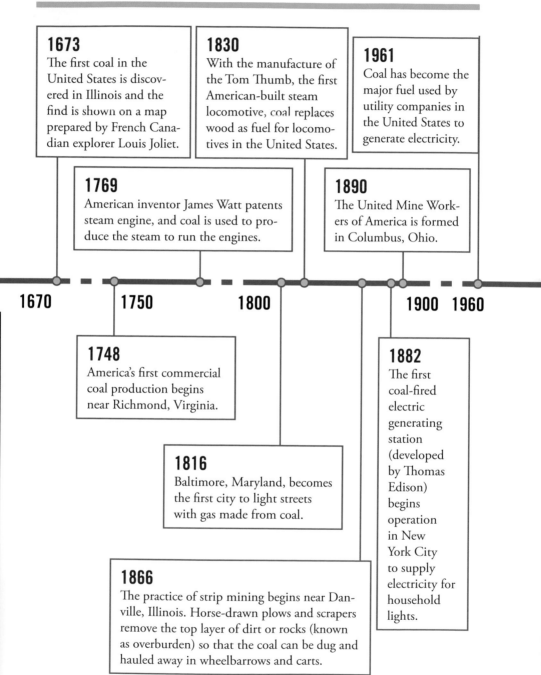

1673
The first coal in the United States is discovered in Illinois and the find is shown on a map prepared by French Canadian explorer Louis Joliet.

1830
With the manufacture of the Tom Thumb, the first American-built steam locomotive, coal replaces wood as fuel for locomotives in the United States.

1961
Coal has become the major fuel used by utility companies in the United States to generate electricity.

1769
American inventor James Watt patents steam engine, and coal is used to produce the steam to run the engines.

1890
The United Mine Workers of America is formed in Columbus, Ohio.

1670   1750   1800   1900   1960

1748
America's first commercial coal production begins near Richmond, Virginia.

1882
The first coal-fired electric generating station (developed by Thomas Edison) begins operation in New York City to supply electricity for household lights.

1816
Baltimore, Maryland, becomes the first city to light streets with gas made from coal.

1866
The practice of strip mining begins near Danville, Illinois. Horse-drawn plows and scrapers remove the top layer of dirt or rocks (known as overburden) so that the coal can be dug and hauled away in wheelbarrows and carts.

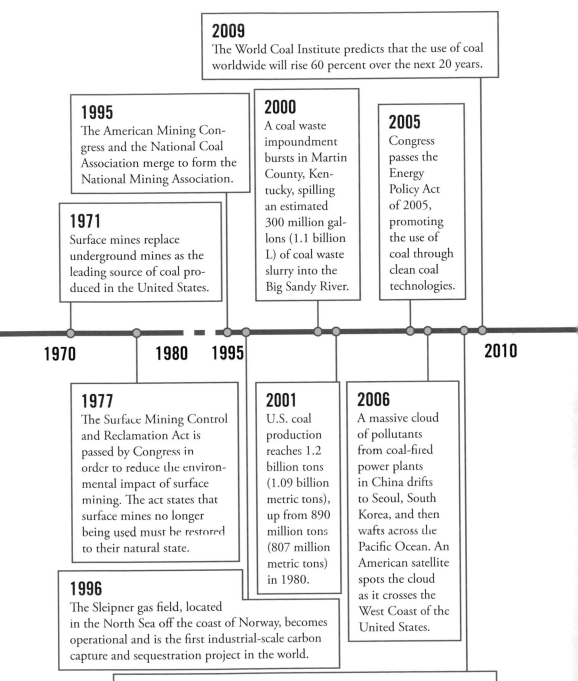

2009
The World Coal Institute predicts that the use of coal worldwide will rise 60 percent over the next 20 years.

1995
The American Mining Congress and the National Coal Association merge to form the National Mining Association.

2000
A coal waste impoundment bursts in Martin County, Kentucky, spilling an estimated 300 million gallons (1.1 billion L) of coal waste slurry into the Big Sandy River.

2005
Congress passes the Energy Policy Act of 2005, promoting the use of coal through clean coal technologies.

1971
Surface mines replace underground mines as the leading source of coal produced in the United States.

1970   1980   1995   2010

1977
The Surface Mining Control and Reclamation Act is passed by Congress in order to reduce the environmental impact of surface mining. The act states that surface mines no longer being used must be restored to their natural state.

2001
U.S. coal production reaches 1.2 billion tons (1.09 billion metric tons), up from 890 million tons (807 million metric tons) in 1980.

2006
A massive cloud of pollutants from coal-fired power plants in China drifts to Seoul, South Korea, and then wafts across the Pacific Ocean. An American satellite spots the cloud as it crosses the West Coast of the United States.

1996
The Sleipner gas field, located in the North Sea off the coast of Norway, becomes operational and is the first industrial-scale carbon capture and sequestration project in the world.

2008
A retaining wall holding back decades worth of coal ash waste bursts at the Kingston Fossil Plant in Harriman, Tennessee, flooding the surrounding residential area with more than 1 billion gallons (4 billion L) of coal ash. It is the worst coal ash disaster in U.S. history.

Related Organizations

American Coal Council

1101 Pennsylvania Ave. NW, Suite 600

Washington, DC 20004

phone: (202) 756-4540 • fax: (732) 231-6581

e-mail: info@americancoalcouncil.org • Web site: www.clean-coal.info

As a representative of the coal industry, this group seeks to advance the development and use of coal and coal technology. Its Web site features fact sheets, book reviews, case studies, *American Coal* magazine, a quarterly newsletter, and a link to a blog.

American Coal Foundation

101 Constitution Ave. NW, Suite 525 East

Washington, DC 20001-2133

phone: (202) 463-9785 • fax: (202) 463-9786

e-mail: info@teachcoal.org • Web site: www.teachcoal.org

As a representative of U.S. coal industries, the foundation develops and distributes coal-related materials and programs. Its "All About Coal" Web site section includes facts on coal and coal regulations, frequently asked questions, and a map of U.S. coal reserves. The site also offers a glossary, news and events, and links to other coal-related sites.

American Coalition for Clean Coal Electricity

PO Box 1638

Alexandria, VA 22313

phone: (877) 358-6699

e-mail: info@americaspower.org • Web site: www.americaspower.org

The American Coalition for Clean Coal Electricity seeks to advance the development and usage of advanced clean coal technologies that will produce electricity with low pollutant emissions. Its Web site features news articles, a facts section, issues and policies, coal reserves information, frequently asked questions, and a link to the Behind the Plug blog.

Environmental Literacy Council

1625 K St. NW, Suite 1020

Washington, DC 20006-3868

phone: (202) 296-0390 • fax: (202) 822-0991

e-mail: info@enviroliteracy.org • Web site: www.enviroliteracy.org

The Environmental Literacy Council offers free information about environmental science to educators, students, policy makers, and the public. Its Web site's search engine produces a number of publications about coal power, including its history, coal mining, effects on the environment, and links to recommended resources for further research.

Greenpeace

702 H St. NW

Washington, DC 20001

phone: (202) 462-1177 • toll-free: (800) 326-0959

e-mail: info@wdc.greenpeace.org • Web site: www.greenpeacc.org

Grccnpeace is an activist organization that works to expose global environmental problems and to propose solutions that help solve those problems. Its Web site offcrs news articles, information about climate change and global warming, a link to the Greenpeace blog, and numerous coal-related publicatious.

National Mining Association

101 Constitution Ave. NW, Suite 500 East

Washingtun, DC 20001

phone: (202) 463-2600 • fax: (202) 463-2666

e-mail: webmaster@nma.org • Web site: www.nma.org

The National Mining Association represents the American mining industry in political, regulatory, legal, and media matters. Its Web site features ncws articles, speeches, the *Mining Week* newsletter, and information about modern mining methods and the importance of coal as an energy source.

Post Carbon Institute

500 N. Main St., Suite 100

Sebastopol, CA 95472

phone: (707) 823-8700 • fax: (866) 797-5820

Web site: www.postcarbon.org

The Post Carbon Institute seeks to help individuals and communities understand and respond to what it perceives as the environmental, societal, and economic crises created by being dependent on fossil fuels. Its Web site features articles, commentaries, reports, a monthly newsletter, news releases, and a section on current and past initiatives.

Sierra Club

85 Second St., 2nd Floor

San Francisco, CA 94105

phone: (415) 977-5500 • fax: (415) 977-5799

e-mail: info@sierraclub.org • Web site: www.sierraclub.org

The Sierra Club is a grassroots environmental movement that opposes the proliferation of coal power because of its effect on the land, air, and water. Numerous publications about coal mining, environmental damage caused by coal power, fact sheets, legislative decisions, the Sierra Club Compass blog, and a video called *Good and Bad News About Coal* are found on its Web site.

Union of Concerned Scientists

Two Brattle Sq.

Cambridge, MA 02238-9105

phone: (617) 547-5552 • fax: (617) 864-9405

Web site: www.ucsusa.org

The Union of Concerned Scientists is a science-based nonprofit organization that works toward a healthy environment and a safer world. Its Web site offers a number of publications related to coal power issues such as air pollution and other environmental effects, waste products, and freshwater depletion.

U.S. Department of Energy Office of Fossil Energy

1000 Independence Ave. SW

Washington, DC 20585

phone: (800) 342-5363 • fax: (202) 586-4403

Web site: http://fossil.energy.gov

The Office of Fossil Energy's primary mission is to ensure that the United States can continue to rely on clean, affordable energy from traditional fuel resources. Its Web site offers information about efforts to protect the air, soil, and water; coal data reports, analyses, and surveys; coal publications; annual energy outlooks; and fact sheets about coal power.

World Coal Institute

5th Floor, Heddon House

149–151 Regent St.

London W1B 4JD

United Kingdom

phone: 44 (0) 20 7851 0052 • fax: 44 (0) 20 7851 0061

e-mail: info@worldcoal.org • Web site: www.worldcoal.org

As an advocate for global coal production, the World Coal Institute seeks to provide a forum for the exchange of information and the discussion of challenges relating to the coal industry. Its Web site offers information about the importance of coal as a global energy source, uses of coal, where coal is found, and environmental impacts, as well as statistics and current news articles.

Worldwatch Institute

1776 Massachusetts Ave. NW

Washington, DC 20036-1904

phone: (202) 452-1999 • fax: (202) 296-7365

e-mail: worldwatch@worldwatch.org • Web site: www.worldwatch.org

The Worldwatch Institute works toward an ecologically sustainable society that meets human needs. Its Web site's search engine produces numerous articles on coal-related issues, from coal power's effect on climate change to the environmental effects of mining and coal burning.

For Further Research

Books

Shirley Stewart Burns, *Bringing Down the Mountains: The Impact of Mountaintop Removal on Southern West Virginia Communities*. Morgantown: West Virginia University Press, 2007.

Jeff Goodell, *Big Coal: The Dirty Secret Behind America's Energy Future*. Boston: Mariner, Houghton Mifflin, 2007.

Richard Heinberg, *Blackout: Coal, Climate and the Last Energy Crisis*. Gabriola Island, BC: New Society, 2009.

Silas House and Jason Howard, *Something's Rising: Appalachians Fighting Mountaintop Removal*. Lexington: University Press of Kentucky, 2009.

Michale Logan, *Coal: Opposing Viewpoints*. Detroit, MI: Greenhaven, 2007.

Joan Quigley, *The Day the Earth Caved In: An American Mining Tragedy*. New York: Random House, 2009.

Michael Shnayerson, *Coal River*. New York: Farrar, Straus & Giroux, 2008.

John Tabak, *Coal and Oil*. New York: Facts On File, 2009.

Periodicals

Robert U. Ayres and Ed Ayres, "A Bridge to the Renewable Energy Future: Renewables Are Coming Fast. In the Meantime, Here's a Largely Overlooked but Potent Way to Minimize Fossil Fuel Use and the Damage It Causes," *World Watch*, September/October 2009.

Economist, "The Writing on the Wall: Coal-Fired Power Plants," May 9, 2009.

Sean Flynn, "Black Tide: Tennessee Valley Authority on the Kingston Fossil Plant," *Gentlemen's Quarterly*, June 2009.

Stephen Fraser, "Coal Case: Another Disastrous Spill Is Prompting

Americans to Ask: How Clean Is Coal?" *Current Science, a Weekly Reader Publication*, May 1, 2009.

Bruce Geiselman, "EPA Lists Hazardous Coal Ash Locations," *Waste & Recycling News*, July 20, 2009.

Jonah Goldberg, "Fossil Future: New Supplies of Oil and Coal Must Be Part of Any Rational Energy Policy," *National Review*, July 6, 2009.

Guy Gugliotta, "Forest Primeval: An Illinois Coal Mine Holds the World's Largest Fossil Wilderness, a Snapshot of Life on Earth 300 Million Years Ago," *Smithsonian*, July 2009.

Todd D. Kantorczyk, "Clean Coal: Is Carbon Sequestration Coming to Pa.?" *Legal Intelligencer*, June 18, 2009.

Christine MacDonald, "Is This the End of Coal? Momentum Is Building to Block New Coal-Fired Power Plants and End Mountaintop Removal Mining. Is There Enough Political Will to Make the Break?" *E: The Environmental Magazine*, September/October 2009.

M.J. Morgan, "Coal—Old Faithful Back in Favour," *African Business*, July 2009.

Mark Rowe, "The Burning Question: It Has Been Described as 'the Single Greatest Threat to Civilisation and All Life on Our Planet', but We Just Can't Seem to Shake Our Dependence on Coal. Indeed, Consumption Is Rising Rapidly, Especially in China, Where It's Being Used to Fuel the Country's Economic Boom. So, Can We Clean Up Coal Before It's Too Late?" *Geographical*, June 2009.

Chuck Soder, "Region Would Feel Effects of Emissions Regulations," *Crain's Cleveland Business*, July 13, 2009.

US Newswire, "EIP Report: Other Toxic Coal Pollution Dumps Around the U.S. Pose Greater Potential Danger than Tennessee Coal Ash Spill Disaster Site," January 7, 2009.

USA Today (magazine), "Coal Remains a Major Player," August 2009.

Internet Sources

Ronald Bailey, "Coal Will Still Be King," *Reason*, January 20, 2009. www.reason.com/news/show/131146.html.

Jeff Biggers, "Fearless Tree-Sit in Coal Blasting Area Calls Out Failed

Regulations," *Huffington Post*, August 25, 2009. www.huffington post.com/jeff-biggers/urgent-911-to-epa-osm-fea_b_268335.html.

Energy Information Administration, "Coal Basics 101," 2008. www.eia. doe.gov/basics/coal_basics.html.

Barbara Freese, Steve Clemmer, and Alan Nogee, "Coal Power in a Warming World," Union of Concerned Scientists, October 2008. www.ucsusa.org/assets/documents/clean_energy/Coal-power-in-a-warming-world.pdf.

David Gelber and Joel Bach, producers, "The Dilemma over Coal Generated Power," *60 Minutes*, April 23, 2009. www.cbsnews.com/stories/2009/04/23/60minutes/main4964301.shtml.

Keith Johnson, "Power Play: Clean Coal, Nukes Key to America's Electricity Future," *Wall Street Journal*, August 4, 2009. http://blogs.wsj.com/environmentalcapital/2009/08/04/power-play-clean-coal-nukes-key-to-americas-electricity-future.

Source Notes

Overview

1. American Coal Council, "What Is Coal?" 2009. www.clean-coal.info.
2. L. Douglas Smoot and Philip J. Smith, *Coal Combustion and Gasification*. New York: Plenum, 1985, p. 111.
3. John Warren, "Court Guts Acid Rain Clean Air Rules," *Adirondack Almanack*, July 15, 2008. www.adirondack almanack.com.
4. Tracy Shapiro, "Investigating Looney Creek: An Ecosystem Autopsy in Which We Suspect Mining as the Cause of Death," *Appalachian Voice*, March 2007. www.appvoices.org.
5. Martin Hoffert, interview with author, October 11, 2008.
6. U.S. Department of Energy, "Cleaning Up Coal: The Clean Coal Technology Program," October 9, 2008. http://fossil.energy.gov.
7. Quoted in Elisabeth Rosenthal, "Europe Turns Back to Coal, Raising Climate Fears," *New York Times*, April 23, 2008. www.nytimes.com.

How Dependent Is the World on Coal Power?

8. Louisa Lim, "China's Coal-Fueled Boom Has Costs," National Public Radio, May 2, 2007. www.npr.org.
9. Quoted in Si Tingting, "Shenhua Shows the Way to Make Gas from Coal," *China Daily*, January 22, 2009. www.chinadaily.com.
10. Caroline Friedman and Teresita Schaffer, "India's Energy Options: Coal and Beyond," *South Asia Monitor*, August 24, 2009. http://csis.org.
11. Steven Mufson and Blaine Harden, "Coal Can't Fill World's Burning Appetite," *Washington Post*, March 20, 2008. www.washingtonpost.com.
12. Quoted in *Your Mining News*, "Technology the Key to Turn Europe's Coal into Clean Energy," September 4, 2009. www.yourminingnews.com.
13. Quoted in Alvin Powell, "Mining Exec: Coal Vital to Energy Mix," *Harvard Gazette*, February 5, 2009. http://news.harvard.edu.
14. World Coal Institute, "Uses of Coal," 2009. www.worldcoal.org.
15. Quoted in Susan Sullivan, "Former WVU Football Coach Speaks About Importance of Coal," WBOY-TV, July 23, 2009. http://wboy.com.

Does Coal Burning Threaten the Environment?

16. Quoted in John Nielsen, "The Killer Fog of '52," National Public Radio, December 11, 2002. www.npr.org.
17. Nielsen, "The Killer Fog of '52."
18. Blacksmith Institute, *The World's Worst Polluted Places*, September 2007. www.blacksmithinstitute.org.
19. David Chandler, "MIT Report Debunks China Energy Myth," *MIT News*, October 6, 2008. http://web.mit.edu.
20. Alice McKeown, *The Dirty Truth About Coal*, Sierra Club, June 2007. www.sierraclub.org.
21. Quoted in Conning Chu, "Early Snowmelt Raises Concerns," *Casper (WY) Star-Tribune*, March 25, 2008. www.trib.com.
22. Union of Concerned Scientists, "Environmental Impacts of Coal Power: Wastes Generated," 2009. www.ucsusa.org.
23. Mike Bryan, "Worst Coal Ash Spill in U.S. History Ruins Huge Area in Ten-

nessee," *Intelligence Daily*, January 12, 2009. www.inteldaily.com.

24. James Hansen, "Global Warming Twenty Years Later: Tipping Points Near," testimony before Congress, June 23, 2008. www.columbia.edu.

25. Quoted in Mark Clayton, "Global Boom in Coal Power—and Emissions," *Christian Science Monitor*, March 22, 2007. www.csmonitor.com.

What Are the Environmental Effects of Coal Mining?

26. Quoted in Kerstin Gehmlich, "Earthquake Shakes Up German Coal Mining," Reuters, March 4, 2008. http://uk.reuters.com.

27. Michael Hendryx and Melissa M. Ahern, "Mortality in Appalachian Coal Mining Regions: The Value of Statistical Life Lost," *Public Health Reports*, July/August 2009. http://wv-gazette.com.

28. Quoted in Charles Duhigg, "Clean Water Laws Are Neglected, at a Cost in Suffering," *New York Times*, September 12, 2009. www.nytimes.com.

29. U.S. Geological Survey, "Coal-Mine Drainage Projects in Pennsylvania," September 30, 2008. http://pa.water.usgs.gov.

30. John McQuaid, "The Razing of Appalachia: Mountaintop Removal Revisited," Environment 360, May 12, 2009. www.e360.yale.edu.

31. American Coal Foundation, "Coal and the Environment: Land and Air," 2007. www.teachcoal.org.

32. Quoted in Ken Ward Jr., "Mine Operators Not Restoring Mountains, OSM Report Finds," *Charleston (WV) Gazette*, July 25, 2009. http://sunday gazettemail.com.

What Is the Future of Coal Power?

33. Quoted in Keith Bradsher, "China Outpaces U.S. in Cleaner Coal-Fired Plants," *New York Times*, May 11, 2009. www.nytimes.com.

34. Gregory H. Boyce, "Common Sense on Energy, Economy, Environment," *Hill*, June 24, 2009. http://thehill.com.

35. David Roberts, "Debate: Roberts v. 'Clean Coal' Flack Joe Lucas," *Huffington Post*, May 14, 2009. www.huffing tonpost.com.

36. U.S. Department of Energy, "Gasification Technology R&D," August 17, 2009. www.fossil.energy.gov.

37. Carbon Capture & Sequestration, "Frequently Asked Questions." www.ccs-education.net.

38. Quoted in CBC News, "Carbon Capture No 'Silver Bullet' for Climate Change," July 3, 2009. www.cbc.ca.

39. CBC News, "Carbon Capture No 'Silver Bullet' for Climate Change."

List of Illustrations

Index